Annie Ashworth and Meg Sanders are a successful writing team who have collaborated on nine non-fiction titles including *Trade Secrets, Trade Secrets Parenting* and *How to Beat the System*, also published by Orion. During their careers they have covered every subject from mortgages to mealy bugs, and fox hunting to fitness. Between them they've notched up at least forty burnt turkeys for their long-suffering families but, undeterred, are still convinced Father Christmas exists.

Trade Secrets
CHRISTMAS

Annie Ashworth
and Meg Sanders

ORION

An Orion paperback

First published in Great Britain in 2001
by Orion
This paperback edition published in 2004
by Orion Books Ltd,
Orion House, 5 Upper St Martin's Lane,
London WC2H 9EA

A CIP catalogue record for this book is available
from the British Library.

ISBN 0 75285 920 X

Printed by LegoPrint, Italy

www.orionbooks.co.uk

Contents

Foreword

It's all over in twenty-four hours, yet we seem to start planning next Christmas from the moment that last piece of wilting mistletoe goes in the bin.

With busy lives, and the commercial pressures that seem to dictate that crackers appear on the shelves sometime in August, it's easy to feel overwhelmed by the pressures that Christmastime brings. More importantly, it's easy to forget just what it's all about: a time for family and friends to get together, for children to be entranced, for work to be put aside and for the contemplation of an amazing birth over two thousand years ago.

To help you shoulder the pressures, we've left no pine cone unturned to bring you every possible tip, scam and downright cheat to achieve the perfect festive celebrations. Whether you are the host or the guest, the cook or the bottle-washer, you'll find here a veritable encyclopaedia of advice, so you'll be able to relax and enjoy the fun that Christmas should be.

We've begged, stolen and borrowed unmercifully and to those we have imposed on, we thank you very much for admitting the secrets of your success. May your baubles sparkle, your turkey be plump and your tree hold on to all its needles.

Cheers!
Annie Ashworth
Meg Sanders

Trade Secrets
CHRISTMAS

Budgeting for Christmas
Annie Page

Try to budget for Christmas throughout the year. Put a little aside each month into a special account and do not dip into it until you need to buy presents and food for the festive season.

Cut the cost of credit card spending by choosing a card with a low interest rate. Deals are often only for a limited period (usually 6 months), so check whether new spending is also at the low rate or just any transferred balance.

Store cards can spread the cost – buy now pay later – but they charge very high interest and try to tempt you at this time of year with special deals like 10 or 20 per cent off all your purchases on the day you sign up for the card. Only sign up if you can pay off the balance as soon as it falls due.

Mail order can spread the cost, but beware! Although you usually do not have to pay interest, prices are often higher than the prices charged in the High Street, and there is postage and packing on top.

Interest-free credit deals in shops and stores may not be all that they seem. The amount that you agree to pay is sometimes less than is necessary to pay off the balance over the interest-free period. At the end of the interest-free period, you will only have repaid around a quarter of the full amount. If you do not pay the balance, your repayments automatically continue and there will be a large interest charge on the whole deal.

If you plan to take on debt, add up everything that you owe at present other than the mortgage. You are safe if the total is equal to 3 months' take-home pay – or less. If the total is higher than 6 months' take-home pay, you should definitely *not* take on more debts.

Be thoughtful, not over-generous. Good presents don't need to be expensive. Set yourself an affordable budget for each person and stick to it.

When you are the host, but finances are tight, ask guests to provide one meal each, or perhaps the booze. This may actually make them feel more comfortable about receiving your hospitality.

Cards and Presents

Buying Presents
Betty Sage; David Wright; Mary French

Make a list and stick to it. Once you are armed with a list of present ideas, it is easier to follow it than wander around vaguely, getting tired and disillusioned.

If you are ordering presents by mail order, make certain that the goods will arrive by Christmas. Twenty-eight days is the longest you will usually be expected to wait.

Shop over the phone. Many companies will deliver by post to the present recipient; smoked salmon and wine, for example.

Save up a day's holiday or ask a sympathetic employer for a morning off, and get your shopping done on a quiet Monday morning when the shops are less busy.

Nip over to France for unusual groceries and presents, and, of course, bottles of interesting wines. A hamper filled with goodies that may be quite run-of-the-mill in France will be a big treat in the UK. There is no restriction to the amount of tobacco, perfumes and alcohol that you can bring back for personal use.

Leave the children behind with someone else at home …

In fact, don't take anyone with you – unless you are incapable of making decisions. You'll get a lot more done on your own and it's important to make it a time for yourself.

When you are out shopping, focus on one age group at a time. Get into children/men/ auntie mode so that you are in the right frame of mind.

Buying in a hurry? Stick to one theme, like books or toiletries.

Don't shop till you drop. Take time out when shopping. It's surprisingly tiring, but stopping every hour or so for a break will keep up your energy levels.

Put your bag under your coat. This is good for security, but it also means that if you get hot, you can take off your coat without having to untangle your bag.

It takes away some of the spontaneity, but ask difficult candidates for a list of presents they'd like. Even if you don't follow to the letter, it'll give you some ideas and point you in the right direction.

Many department stores – Debenhams, House of Fraser, Marks and Spencer – offer a free personal shopper service if you are really stuck for inspiration.

Start at the top of a department store and work your way down. That way, you won't be carrying heavy parcels up stairs.

If friends or family have birthdays around Christmas, it's not fair to amalgamate two lots of presents into one. Give them a gift token, but buy birthday cards well in advance, as shops tend to take their selections of these off display to make room for Christmas cards.

Buying someone a mobile phone for Christmas? Make sure it is up and running before you wrap it, so that they can use it straight away. You could even dial the number just as they are about to open the parcel!

The same applies to computers. Download the essential software so that the recipient can get going straight away. You don't want to be phoning helplines on Christmas Day.

When you're setting up the new computer, there are a few things to remember:

- *Position the seat* relative to the desk so that you don't use your mouse with your arm straight and your elbow locked – it can cause damage to your elbow.
- *Angle the screen* so that there are no troublesome reflections from windows or lights.
- *Be very careful* with magnets around computers. If a magnet comes into contact with your screen, the image can become completely distorted, and magnets can wipe floppy disks or other electronic hardware.

If you're getting rid of old computers, bear in mind that they could be of use to other people. An organisation that would be grateful for unwanted computers is:

- *Computers for Charities:*
  for UK donations call 01323 840641.
  www.computersforcharities.co.uk

Make sure you have plenty of batteries. When batteries are fading, a little more life can be squeezed out of them if you warm them on a radiator.

Tighten loose batteries by pushing in a wedge of thin foil at one end of the battery casing. The foil from a bar of chocolate is ideal. (Now *there's* an excuse to buy a bar!)

Have pen and paper handy and make a list of presents as they are opened.

Tactful way to say something isn't right? Suggest that you already have one (you thought it was such a good idea) …

Or keep mum and, if you can, return the item to the shop where it was bought after Christmas. Many stores will exchange goods without a receipt if you explain that you want an exchange.

Consumer Rights
Citizens' Advice Bureau

When ordering over the Internet, ensure the site has ordering security.

Don't forget to post off the guarantee cards that come with items like electrical goods, or they won't be valid.

Beware when buying goods on extended credit. If you want to cancel the agreement – for example, because you can no longer afford the goods – you will only be able to change your mind about keeping them if:
- **the goods were bought at your home** and the order is cancelled within a short period; *or*
- **the seller agrees to cancel the sale.** Some sellers do this, others may provide a credit note instead of a cash refund; *or*
- **the agreement contains cancellation clauses.** These will set out whether and when cancellation is allowed and may also set out any charges payable on cancellation.

You may be able to claim compensation if you told the seller that you needed goods delivered by a certain date and they were not delivered on time. If no specified date was given, then you must give the seller a date by which you expect the goods to be delivered before taking any further action.

Bull in a china shop? You are liable to pay for any goods or property of the shop that become damaged by you or your children. If the goods are damaged by accident, it may be the shop's responsibility, since the seller has a duty to take care to protect goods from foreseeable accidents.

Refunds and replacements

Unsure a present will be right? Many shops offer gift receipts on which an actual value doesn't appear. The recipient can then return the goods and exchange them for something more suitable.

Find out how long a period you have in which to return something to the shop. This is important if you are an early Christmas shopper and you think a gift might need changing.

Keep all your Christmas receipts in an envelope, so that you can find them easily if you need to return an item to a store.

Decide you don't like a gift after all? You will only be able to change it, have a credit note or obtain a refund if this was agreed at the time of the sale with the seller. Check before you buy if you aren't sure.

Unsure if an item is the right size or colour? Check the shop's policy. Shops are not legally bound to take something back unless it is faulty.

Faulty goods

When presents do turn out to be faulty, you have the right to insist on a refund rather than a credit note. You should return them to the shop, with the receipt, and you will be entitled to some or all of your money back.

Check your credit card small print. Many credit card companies offer free cover against loss, theft or accidental damage on items worth over £50.

If the seller has already pointed out stains, chips, cracks, etc., you cannot complain about defects afterwards.

Unsolicited goods

An irritating parcel arrives that you didn't order. You do not have to pay for these goods or send them back. Either:

- **write to the sender,** saying that you did not order the goods. Give your name and the address at which the goods can be collected and, if necessary, say how collection can be arranged. The sender then has 30 days to collect the goods. If the sender does not collect within this period, the goods become your property; *or*
- **do nothing,** but keep the goods safe for 6 months. If the sender fails to collect them within this time, they become your property.

If you receive an invoice or letter asking for payment for goods that were not ordered, either ignore it or report the matter to the local trading standards as the sender may have committed a criminal offence. Try complaining in writing to the sender too.

A Good Send-off
Monica Shaw, Linda Blackwood; The Post Office

Mail should always be clearly addressed and include the postcode. Customers can call 0845 7111222 (calls are charged at local rates) for the postcode of any UK address. Alternatively, visit the Royal Mail website at www.royalmail.com.

Place stamps at the top right-hand corner of the envelope or package because this is where the sorting machinery automatically looks for them.

Sorting machinery automatically searches for the postcode on the last line of an address so make sure the postcode is there.

Commas and full stops can confuse optical character-recognition machinery, so don't use them when addressing an item.

Don't use 'near' or 'by' in an address. It can confuse sorting machinery. The postcode is enough to ensure the item gets through.

Putting the sender's address in small print on the back of an item, whether a card or a parcel, helps the return of any items that the Royal Mail cannot deliver without it having to be opened.

Always seal envelopes. There is no cheaper rate for unsealed envelopes.

If stamps or gummed labels get stuck together, cover them with a sheet of paper and press them gently with a warm iron. They should separate easily.

Cards

Make your own cards using watercolour paper. Give cards a deckle edge by painting a line with water, letting it soak in and then pulling the card apart along the line. Use a dismantled envelope as a template for the size of paper you need. To decorate, use foil from sweet wrappers or amaretti biscuit wrappers (flatten them out with the pad of your finger), and stick on glass beads, ivy leaves, or torn scraps from old documents.

Doing your own posting? Some letterbox flaps are sprung to seal in the heat. They can really snap on your fingers and cause a lot of pain. Avoid this by using both hands to post cards. Push the flap open with one hand and push the card through with the other.

Before you throw cards away after Christmas, make sure you've made a note of people you have received cards from, as well as those you forgot, to include them on your list for next year, together with new addresses and new children!

Sending parcels

If you are sending valuable items, always send them by recorded or registered post, and keep the receipt. In the unlikely event that they go missing, you will then have some evidence for compensation.

Mail should always be well wrapped to prevent:
- *it being lost*
- *damage* to the contents or to other mail
- *injury* to the postman or recipient

To keep delicate presents safe when sending them through the post, pack gaps in the box with recycled egg boxes – break them up to fit if you need to.

For larger items, use cartons that are appropriate for the weight of the item to be sent. The boxes that goods are sold in are not always suitable for mailing, without extra packaging or stiffening.

Mark the weight of heavy items on the box to help avoid lifting injuries.

Strong tape should be used to cover all openings to prevent them from catching on other items.

Flatten any metal fastenings or staples and cover with tape to prevent them causing injury or snagging on other items.

For packing, use polystyrene chips, polyethylene foam sheeting, bubble wrap, shredded paper (inland only), moulded polystyrene blocks, crushed or corrugated paper or wood wool.

Padded envelopes are perfect for paperback books but for larger or hardback books use a corrugated fibreboard book pack with 25mm clearance at the ends.

CDs, cassettes and computer disks should be packed in material that will protect the item from magnetic fields. Use either a rigid purpose-made container or wrap the item in at least a 20mm thickness of soft packaging.

Films should be individually labelled with the sender's name and address, and should be packed in a strong envelope.

Make sure that tins or bottles containing liquids and creams, such as cosmetics, are sealed with tape, wrapped in polythene, sealed again and then packed with absorbent material, such as sawdust or newspaper, in a fibreboard or polystyrene container.

Powders such as cosmetics or bath salts are best sealed first in a strong polythene bag and then placed in a rigid corrugated board box.

When packing framed pictures, make sure each one is sandwiched between 2 pieces of hardboard or 2 polystyrene slabs that overlap each side by at least 25mm. At least 50mm of soft packing should be placed between the frame and the boards.

Empty cling film tubes are great for sending pictures, posters or calendars.

Polystyrene chippings are a nuisance to

dispose of, but they can be useful to gardeners. When potting up containers, place a layer in the bottom before you start adding compost; it makes the pot lighter and therefore much easier to move.

Festive Food and Drink

Food at Christmas
Radcliffe Catering; ASDA; Leonard Goode, Safeways

If possible, find a butcher who will deliver your turkey on Christmas Eve. You can then leave it (well wrapped and covered) somewhere cool overnight until it is ready to cook and it won't take up precious room in a packed fridge.

At the supermarket

Supermarkets are least busy in the evenings early on in the week. The nearer Christmas is to the weekend, the busier the shops will be later on in the week as people get into a weekend frame of mind.

When you go to the supermarket, make sure you buy food with the longest 'use by' date. These items are usually packed at the back of the shelves.

Buy larger packs of non-perishable items well in advance, and leave the perishables until the last minute.

If your trolley has a wobbly wheel, don't suffer in silence. It'll only get worse as you add more shopping, so ask an assistant to get you a better one. If you use a faulty one, inform the bag packers at the end – they'll arrange to send it for repair.

Open those pesky plastic bags by placing them between your hands, held together in a prayer position, then rub your hands back and forth against each other. The bag should open easily.

If you're packing heavy or sharp items, such as bacon in plastic trays, take the precaution of popping one bag inside another before you start to put them in.

If a bag does split while you're packing, put it down, open another bag and pop the whole thing inside, keeping the handles together at the top.

Pack household cleaning products separately. Even if they don't leak, they still have a strong perfume that can taint food.

Always pack cooked and uncooked food separately, and keep them apart in the fridge too.

When packing a trolley, bag or plastic box, make a foundation at the bottom of heavy items, such as spuds or tins, and lay lighter things on top.

The most crushable items go right on top – flowers, bread, eggs, grapes, berries and light veg, so buy them last, whatever the layout of the supermarket.

Iced cakes must stay on top. Even a light item laid on top will cause the plastic to stick to the icing and ruin the whole thing.

Bottles are amazingly heavy – no more than two to a bag. Double up the bag if you put in a third bottle.

Keep bottles upright in trolleys and in bags. They are much less likely to break this way if put down with a bump than if they are on their sides.

Bottles are best put upright on the conveyor belt at the checkout. If you put them on their sides, be sure to wedge them in place, or they're likely to roll.

Baguettes are a real nightmare. To keep them in one piece, stand them up in the corner of a deep trolley. In a shallow trolley, buy them last and lay them across the top of the other shopping (but not iced cakes: see above).

Plastic boxes call for a different technique. Loaded, they can be really heavy. Try to distribute heavy and light things evenly between boxes to keep the weight about equal.

Make sure you've got the right trolley for the plastic boxes before you start.

Check you haven't left anything behind on the till. Wrapped deli snacks are easy to miss among the spare bags.

Order online for delivery, or some stores will let you reserve and collect.

Getting ahead

Make brandy butter weeks ahead. Freeze scoops of it on a tray, then pack in a container. Thaw in the fridge for 45 minutes.

Foods that you can freeze ahead include: cooked rice, milk in plastic or waxed-paper containers (semi-skimmed or skimmed, but not whole milk), whipping cream (whisk thoroughly when it has defrosted), fresh pasta, bread, bacon, butter, stuffing, pastry and mince pies.

Chop up fresh herbs and freeze them in ice trays so that you can pop them out when required.

Cook braised cabbage the night before it is needed and reheat it in the microwave. It actually tastes better when the flavours have developed.

If you are making a dish for the family, like a casserole or lasagne a few weeks before Christmas, make double the quantity and put it in the freezer in case unexpected guésts drop in over the Christmas period.

Potatoes can be peeled the day before and left in water covered with a slice of bread until you are ready to use them. However, other vegetables will lose their nutrients if peeled too far in advance.

You can even parboil potatoes and parsnips the day before, then leave them (out of their water) somewhere cool, covered. They'll be quicker to cook and crisper on Christmas Day.

Save time later in the day by making sauces up to two days ahead (brandy sauce, bread sauce, custard, etc.) and storing them in thermos flasks until you need them.

Make your own hot chocolate mix so that it's always ready. Combine about 3 parts good-quality cocoa powder, 4 parts vanilla sugar, 7 parts low-fat milk powder and a pinch of cinnamon. Make up with water or milk and water for a warming treat.

Seafood
Oliver Simms

Oysters, which are traditional in France for Christmas dinner, are a real treat and make a good light starter before turkey with all the trimmings.

For sheer quality and for eating raw, go for the round, flat common oyster. Cheaper Portuguese oysters are teardrop-shaped with a deeper, lower shell. The gradings are for size – from 1 to 4, with 1 being the largest and 4 the smallest.

Choose oysters with tightly closed shells.

Live oysters in the shell can be kept for about 7–10 days in a cool place.

Don't soak oyster shells in water or scrub them; just rinse off any mud and pick them over.

An oyster knife is a bit of an extravagance, but it's better than spending Christmas Day in casualty.

To open, hold the shell in a thick glove (a leather gardening glove is ideal) or in a folded-up tea towel. Insert the tip of the blade close to the hinge and prise the shell open by twisting. Cut the muscle from the upper shell and discard. Use the oyster knife to loosen the muscle from the lower shell. Place the lower shells with the oyster on ice to serve.

A good serving on the half-shell is 4–6 oysters.

Scallops are also at their best in winter. They don't have to be alive when cooked, but always check for a sweet smell when choosing.

To use the hollow undershells of fresh scallops as serving containers, scrub them thoroughly, then boil in water for 5 minutes.

Keep Coquilles St Jacques from tipping up while you're cooking them by balancing the shells on muffin tins.

Use an oyster knife to open clams. Hold the clam shell using a folded tea towel, with the hinged part of the clam towards your wrist. Hold the clam over a bowl, then insert the knife blade between the shell halves near

the hinge and twist to coax the shell open.
Sever the muscle to release the clam from the
shell and slide the clam into the bowl along
with the nectar.

You can also open clams in a microwave.
After scrubbing, place the clams in a single
layer on a microwaveable dish lined with
paper towels. Cover tightly with cling film
and cook on high for about 1 minute, until
the clams open just slightly. Remove as soon
as this happens and finish opening them by
hand, then refrigerate immediately.

Cheese
Paxton & Whitfield at London, Stratford-upon-Avon and Bath

Serve each cheese with a different knife
so the flavours don't mix.

**Arrange the cheeseboard 1 hour before
serving**, cover and store in a cool place (but
not the fridge).

If you are offering bread, flash heat it in
the oven at 180° or under a hot grill for a
couple of minutes.

Serve unsalted butter. Salted butter can
dilute the taste of cheese.

**Whole cheeses keep better than sliced
ones**, so when you buy a portion of cheese,
eat it as soon as possible.

Large pieces of cheese keep better than
small ones.

Some cheeses like to be kept cold, others prefer a warmer atmosphere. It depends on the cheese and its stage of maturity. No cheese likes temperatures above 20°C or below 4°C. Most are happy between 8°C and 15°C.

Keep your cheese in the salad drawer at the bottom of the fridge, where it is slightly warmer and the confined space maintains humidity. Don't keep salad in the same drawer, however, as salad leaves can pose a hygiene threat to the cheese.

In warmer temperatures a cheese will continue to mature. Reduce the temperature to slow down the maturing process. Hard cheeses are more resilient to temperature extremes. Soft cheeses generally prefer a temperature around 12°C.

Nearly all cheeses like a moist atmosphere, but not too damp – a cool cellar is ideal. If you aren't lucky enough to have one, cover your cheese with a damp cloth, or keep it in a container that stops the moisture escaping, such as a cheese bell or cardboard box.

If the atmosphere is too dry, a cheese will crack. Too damp, and white rind or mould will form.

Waxed paper will keep the cheese in the right condition. It allows the cheese to breathe but not to dry out.

Kitchen foil is ideal for storing blue cheeses.

Don't use cling film around cheese – it tends to allow moisture to build up, encouraging mould.

Unpasteurised cheeses retain more calcium and vitamins than pasteurised ones, but unpasteurised and soft cheeses should be avoided by pregnant women, the very elderly, the very young and those with a depressed immune system.

Always bring cheese to room temperature 1–2 hours before serving.

If you only need a small amount of cheese, buy 1 or 2 good cheeses rather than a wide choice of different cheeses.

For interest, either serve a variety of cheeses (one hard, one soft, a blue cheese and a goat or sheep's cheese) or serve a selection from one geographical area.

Stilton and port is a classic match, but try Wensleydale or Caerphilly with white port, Brie de Meaux with late bottled vintage port and a hard sheep's cheese like Berkswell with 10-year-old tawny port.

Stilton makers say: cut high, cut low, cut level. This means: cut a slice right across the top, 5cm (a couple of inches) down, and leave this disc-shaped slice on top of the cheese. Then cut wedge shapes out of it as if it were a cake. This exposes the least amount of cheese to the air.

Poultry and Game
Sheila Rowley

For a small group, a whole turkey is a bit of a waste – small ones don't have much flavour. Instead, try guinea fowl or capon.

Duck is deceptive because the weight of the bone is high relative to that of the meat. You'll need a much heavier duck than, say, a chicken to feed the same number of people. For 4 people, you need to reckon on a duck of 2.4kg (5lb).

Goose is popular at Christmas and is often free range. Choose a light skin, plump breast and pliable backbone. Old birds can get very tough!

Goose fat – and there is usually plenty of it – is worth keeping to use for frying potatoes or eggs. There will be fat deposits inside the cavity. Remove them before cooking and, if you have enough, try rendering them over a low heat. Fat from poultry can be heated to a high temperature before it burns.

Goose fat is also excellent as a hand cream and for chilblains!

Game is a tasty and low-fat alternative to turkey. One pheasant will feed 2 people; a partridge just 1 person.

Age is critical for game – over 6 months old and they will be inedibly tough if roasted. To test for age (although this is not infall-ible), look for a soft, plump breast and check the feet – if they are scarred and calloused, the bird is likely to be old.

A flexible breastbone is often a sign of a young bird, as are short spurs on a cock bird.

Free-range turkeys can be identified by a good layer of fat under the skin, firm meat, calluses on the feet and, sadly, a far higher price!

To save storage space, put the turkey in a picnic cool box, and leave it outside with the lid on for up to twenty-four hours. Don't pack it with ice, as it will freeze.

When choosing a turkey, look for unbroken skin with no dark patches, and a plump breast.

Make sure you know if there are giblets inside; for incomparable gravy and a great treat for your cat, nothing else will do.

Dealing with whole birds

If you have to remove giblets yourself, have a stiff drink first, then insert your forefinger into the neck end and waggle it around against the bone to loosen everything. With the breast side up, enlarge the tail cavity by making a slit, then insert your finger at that end and waggle, as before. Now the tricky bit: try to pull out all of the innards in one go through the tail end. Take particular care not to break the gall bladder – the green thing attached to the liver – or it will taint the meat.

The giblets may include lungs, heart, liver, gall bladder, gizzard and, in game birds, the intestines. Get rid of the lungs and intestines. Very carefully, cut the gall bladder away from the liver and discard.

The gizzard should be split with a sharp knife, and the crop (a tough membrane) should be cut out and discarded.

Check inside the tail cavity, with the bird breast down, for oil glands and cut them out.

Heart, liver, gizzard and neck can all be cooked to make stock or stuffing.

Remove tubes and membrane from the liver of poultry and game and either sauté on their own for a treat on toast, or include them in the stuffing.

If the liver is very dark, smells strong or is tinged green from the gall bladder, don't use it.

Preparation

To minimise the risk of problems with salmonella (all poultry is susceptible), make sure frozen birds are completely thawed before roasting. All birds should be brought to room temperature before cooking.

Wipe the bird inside and out before cooking to remove as much moisture as possible.

Little bits of quill can be removed from the skin with tweezers.

To remove those little tufts of down, hold the bird taut over an open flame to singe them off. Keep turning the bird – you don't want a barbecue!

To get the sinews out of the legs, first find your sinews. Cut a slit below them and slide a knife sharpener underneath. Twist it until they first snap and then are drawn out of the leg meat.

Pheasant pluckers? Make it easier by dipping your hands in water before you start.

Start on the breast and work upwards to the neck, then turn the bird round and work towards the tail feathers. Turn it over, then do the back; stretch the wings out and pluck the wing feathers. Cut off the pinions where the quills grow, then take out the tail feathers.

Pull out the feathers in the direction in which they grow, not against it.

If feathers are hard to remove, try dipping the bird in just-boiled water for 30 seconds, but you must go on to cook it as soon as you have finished plucking.

Stuffing should be loosely packed and only in the neck end. Alternatively, cook your stuffing in a tray or formed into balls, and leave the bird empty.

For added flavour, pop a peeled onion into the bird cavity, or a lemon cut in quarters, or a preserved lemon.

Cooking a Turkey
Natalie Soames; The Royal Oak Farm Shop; Jenny Walton

Cooking a turkey for several hours means that you have to get up early and the meat ends up dry. Cook it fast as you would any joint.

Stuffing a turkey can make the cooking time much longer. Instead, make up your stuffing, cook it separately and just put a whole onion in the turkey cavity.

If you do stuff the turkey, weigh it after stuffing to calculate the correct cooking time. A stuffed turkey will need plenty of basting to retain the moisture in the breast meat. Let the bird come to room temperature before you put it in the oven or it will take longer to cook.

Use bread that has been reduced in price to stuff your turkey. It's already stale and is much cheaper.

Use dental floss (not the mint-flavoured kind!) to tie up and stitch your turkey.

Wrap the turkey in cooking net (available from supermarkets and cookware shops) to keep in the moisture. It will brown through the net. Cut off the net with scissors before carving.

Lay the turkey on its breast so that the juices run into the breast and keep it moistened while it is cooking.

Cooking times for turkeys:

Cook a fresh turkey at 220°C (425°F, gas mark 7) for the first hour.

Reduce the temperature to 190°C (375°F, gas mark 5) for the remaining time.

Allow 15 minutes per 450g (1lb) for turkeys up to 5.4kg (12lb) in weight.

For turkeys over 5.4kg (12lb), allow another 12 minutes per 450g (1lb).

If cooking uncovered, baste frequently.

Using an Aga? If you are cooking your turkey in the simmering oven, make sure the temperature is above 63°C, having blasted it in the hot oven for 20 minutes first. Otherwise it will be a breeding ground for bacteria.

Open the oven door as little as possible. You won't need to baste your turkey if it is covered in foil.

Unexpected guests? There is enough slack in the skin of a turkey to slip in a couple of chicken breasts and secure them with a cocktail stick.

To check the turkey is cooked, pierce the flesh between the leg and the body. The juices should run clear, not pink. Cover with foil and leave to rest for 30 minutes before carving.

To make carving easier, remove the legs first and then slice the breast.

Taking out the wishbone makes it easier to carve too.

For perfect slices, start carving at an angle above the wing.

Gravy

Thin gravy? Mix some butter with a little flour into a paste and drop it into the simmering gravy. Stir and repeat until it is thick enough.

Instant mashed potato will also thicken gravy a treat.

Alternatively, mix 1 teaspoonful of arrowroot or cornflour with cold water and add to the gravy off the heat, stirring all the time.

Remove excess fat from your gravy by dropping in a few ice cubes. The fat will solidify around them and you can spoon them out easily.

The Trimmings
British Potato Council; Carol Devonshire, Bath Spa Hotel; Lynne Weller; Adele Legroux

When baking a ham, baste it with Coca-Cola. It will make the ham sweet and delicious.

Sausages can be fiddly to turn in the oven. Thread several of them on to a skewer, and you can then simply turn over the skewer halfway through cooking.

Sausages shouldn't need pricking. If they explode, they are being cooked too quickly. As with a steak, seal them, then cook them on a lower heat.

Mush up onion into bread sauce for added flavour – but if you've added cloves to the onion, make sure you remove them first.

Leave out a bowl of nuts (don't forget the nutcracker) for guests to help themselves. But remember that brazil nuts contain 20 times as much fat as chestnuts.

To peel chestnuts: either slit the shells on the rounded side and put them in a gentle oven for 15 to 20 minutes, or sprinkle them with water and bake in a very hot oven for 10 minutes.

If nuts are difficult to crack, try freezing them first. Alternatively, put them in cold water and bring them to the boil for a few minutes.

Vegetables

When space is short for storing vegetables, wrap them in newspaper, place in a carrier bag and peg them on the washing line. They will stay cool and be inaccessible to birds and mice.

If room is short for cooking veg, you can double up parsnips with potatoes and carrots with sprouts.

Refresh frozen veg by rinsing with boiling water before you cook them. It removes the frozen water around them and improves the taste no end.

To cook two veg at once, put one veg in the pan and put a colander containing the other veg on top with a lid. They will be cooked (and steamed) at the same time.

To keep vegetables warm (but not the roast potatoes), drain them, return to the saucepan, wrap it in a blanket and put it in bed under the duvet!

Cook vegetables together as a mixture (carrots and parsnips, peas and beans/sprouts for example). It will help you to get the quantities right.

ROOT VEGETABLES

Some root veg, such as carrots, turnips and onions, have quite a lot of natural sweetness. Bring this out by adding a pinch of sugar when you cook them, and reduce the cooking liquid to a syrupy glaze with a good slice of butter towards the end of the cooking time.

Turnips go off faster than other veg, so don't add them to soups or purées unless you are using them the same day.

Make a tasty gratin of root veg, rather as you would for potatoes. Slice thinly and layer in an ovenproof dish, then pour over a mixture of milk and cream to cover. Bake in a medium oven for about 1 hour.

Glam up roast potatoes. Make a crunchy coating of breadcrumbs (crisped up in the oven), mixed with garlic salt or paprika. Toss parboiled potatoes in this before roasting.

The secret of crispy roast potatoes: once they have been parboiled for about 5 minutes, drain well and put the lid back on the pan. Shake vigorously to fluff up the edges. Pour the potatoes on to very hot fat, and once they are cooked (for about 1 hour at 220°C, 425°F, gas mark 7), serve straight away.

For extra-tasty roast potatoes, make a hole through the potato with an apple corer and push a piece of rolled-up bacon inside, then roast as usual.

When cooking more than 1kg (2lb) potatoes, allow them an extra 15 minutes to brown.

Add unpeeled cloves of garlic to roasting potatoes for extra flavour.

Making mash too? Use hot milk, which makes mashed potatoes lighter and fluffier.

SPROUTS

You can prepare your sprouts on Christmas Eve to save time on the big day. Store in a plastic bag with a little water in the salad section of the fridge.

Cut a little cross in the base of sprouts to reduce cooking time.

Sprouts that are bitter are just awful. The best thing to do with them is make a purée. Cook until tender, then liquidise in a food processor with a little turkey stock, some soured cream, a little nutmeg and a pinch of caster sugar.

Overcooked sprouts are ghastly. Boil in salted water for no more than 8–10 minutes, or steam for about 15 minutes for tender perfection. To microwave, place in a single layer in a dish, cover tightly and cook; 175g (6oz) sprouts take a mere 2 minutes, 350g (12oz) just 3 minutes.

Hate the smell of sprouts and cabbage cooking? Add a good sprig of parsley or a couple of bay leaves to the saucepan while you're boiling them – the flavour won't be affected but the smell will be minimised.

A good squeeze of lemon added to the cooking water will also reduce nasty cabbagey and sprouty smells.

Mix fried bacon and onion with your sprouts to make them tastier.

For sprouts with attitude, toss after cooking in a dressing of lemon juice and olive oil with a little grated lemon zest, parsley and grainy mustard.

Raw sprouts make a healthy salad with crunchy bacon, Chinese leaf and chopped hazelnuts with a mustardy dressing.

If sprouts are banned in your house, the best winter greens are Savoy cabbage, red cabbage and kale.

COOKING FOR VEGETARIANS

Roast the vegetables separately from the meat so that everyone can enjoy them.

Vegetarian festive food: butter a large ramekin, and thinly layer with sliced potatoes, sliced onion and grated cheese. Season. Finish with a layer of potatoes, bake in the oven for about an hour at 160°C and top with cranberry sauce.

Another delicious vegetarian festive recipe: caramelise carrots, parsnips and onions in olive oil in the oven. Then put the veg into a baking tin and top with shortcrust pastry. Bake for 30–40 minutes at 160°C and turn out when cooked for a quick vegetable tarte tatin.

Mince Pies

Val Buchanan, Old Monastery Restaurant, Morayshire; Jon Ainsworth, chef, Snowshill Manor, Worcestershire; Lizzie Evans

If you have made your mincemeat a few weeks in advance, turn the jar on its head for half an hour before you make your mince pies. The brandy will run down and moisten the fruit at the top of the jar.

Add a spoonful of custard powder to mince pie pastry and the result will be golden yellow.

Sprinkle mince pies with caster sugar as soon as they come out of the oven. It will stick on that way.

For a special festive taste, mix icing sugar and cinnamon to sieve over mince pies.

Make lighter pastry for mince pies by using self-raising flour instead of plain.

Also for a rich, light pastry, use hard margarine and add an egg to the mixture, together with 30g (1oz) sugar to every 225g (8oz) flour.

When making pastry, keep a couple of freezer bags close by to slip over your hands in case the phone rings or the doorbell goes.

But don't be too heroic. Pastry is brilliant when made in a food processor, as it prevents it becoming overworked.

Freeze uncooked mince pies, and then take out however many you need, defrost and bake. To bake from frozen, cook for about 40 minutes.

Christmas Pudding
Paul Snazell, Westover Hall Hotel; Jill Brand; Gerry Wallace

Get going early. Christmas puddings are best made well in advance (make next year's and eat last year's) and they can last for up to 3 years.

Keep a Christmas pudding moist by soaking it in stout.

Wrap lucky charms in kitchen foil to stop them tainting the pudding. Make a note of how many have been included and leave it on top of the stored pudding.

Bring your Christmas pud to the boil in a pan half full of water and steam for 30 minutes on top of the cooker, then transfer to a low oven, still in the pan of water, for 12 hours. In this way, your kitchen won't be steamed up. On Christmas Day do the same, leaving it in a low oven for just 2 hours.

Get your pudding ablaze by warming a ladleful of brandy over a flame, pouring it over the pudding, then lighting it. Never let it boil, though, or the flame will not burn for long enough.

Stick a sugar lump into the top of the pudding before you pour the brandy over and it will stay lit longer.

Put a little sugar into the brandy sauce to stop a film forming on the top.

An alternative Christmas pud: layer mincemeat, liqueur, whipped cream and pre-baked meringue.

For the easiest Christmas dessert in the world, drain a can of unsweetened puréed chestnuts. Add about half as much by weight of plain chocolate, 1 cup of water, and about 200g (7oz) each of butter and caster sugar. Mash the chestnuts with a fork, melt together the chocolate and water, beat the butter and sugar together, then combine everything. Spoon into a lined cake tin and chill overnight. Serve cut into very thin slices with whipped cream.

Brandy butter will store in the fridge for 2–3 weeks, and freezes beautifully. Make it tastier by using soft brown sugar instead of white.

The Christmas Cake
Wendy Hicks, Imaginative Icing; Julie Weiner; Jane Asher; Carolyn Bruce-Moore, Top Tier, Stratford-upon-Avon

Condition new cake tins by applying vegetable oil, then baking in a medium oven for about 15 minutes.

For a moister fruit cake in electric ovens or Agas, before turning on the oven, place a baking tin or Pyrex bowl in the bottom, containing 2 pints (40 fl oz) water. This will create a moist atmosphere and produce a better cake.

When adding cherries to your Christmas cake, stop them falling to the bottom by dusting them with flour and warming them in the oven a little before adding them to the cake mixture.

Better still, wash the syrup off the cherries.

Soak dried fruit overnight in a little sherry or rum. Use 1 dessertspoon of alcohol for each 500g (1lb) of fruit.

Dried fruit for a Christmas cake is far tastier if soaked in brandy for 3 days before you bake it. Stir every 12 hours.

Chop dates in a food processor or mincer

before adding to the mix. The resulting cake will be much moister.

Before measuring out treacle or golden syrup, sprinkle the scale dish with flour. The syrup will come out easily.

Peel citrus fruits with a potato peeler before squeezing and drop the rind into a jar containing golden syrup for a tasty addition to cakes.

Place pared orange peel in a low oven until it dries out. Crush and keep in a jar, then add to cakes with the dry ingredients.

Blanch your own almonds by pouring boiling water over them. After a few minutes, drain and squeeze. The skins will come off easily.

To stop your cake rising, make an indentation by pressing down in the middle with the back of a spoon before it goes in the oven. It will come out nice and flat.

Cover your cake in the oven with an old metal biscuit tin. The steam underneath will produce a lovely, moist cake.

It is best not to store Christmas cakes in a tin – there's too much air; wrap instead in a plastic bag or greaseproof paper and tin foil to keep the moisture in.

Simple cakes are often the most stunning, so always work and design to your own capabilities.

Don't throw away cake boards. You can re-cover them with silver or gold paper for another time, and even if one side gets scored by knife cuts, you can turn it over and use the other. You should get 4 goes out of a board, at the very least. If you're careful with your knife, they'll go on for ages.

Marzipan

When covering your cake in almond paste, leave it for at least a day before decorating with icing.

Marzipan can be sticky to roll out. Put it inside a plastic freezer bag or between 2 pieces of cling film or sheets of aluminium foil and then roll it out.

Royal icing

When separating eggs, crack the egg in half on the rim of a glass. Pour the egg yolk from one half of the shell to the other, back and forth, until the white runs down into the glass below and only the yolk is left in the shell.

A little glycerine in royal icing makes it easier to cut.

Icing sets more quickly if made up with boiling water.

Put a tiny amount of blue food colouring into royal icing and it will be whiter than white.

For ready-to-roll icing, you will need:

- 450g (14oz) for a cake 12.5cm (5in) square or 15cm (6in) round.
- 900g (2lb) for a cake 18cm (7in) square or 20.5cm (8in) round.
- 1.4kg (3lb) for a cake 23cm (9in) square or 25.5cm (10in) round.

When rolling out your Christmas cake icing, use cornflour on the board instead of flour, as it isn't abrasive and won't pit the icing.

Don't add icing sugar when you are rolling the icing, either. It will dry it out and make it more likely to crack.

If your icing cracks as you put it on the cake, massage it with the palm of your hand.

If you find the icing slides off your cake, try dusting the cake lightly with flour before you ice it.

Smoothing icing with water will make it very sticky and unmanageable. Instead, smooth icing out by rubbing it with icing sugar.

When making small icing decorations, keep the amount of paste that you use to a minimum.

Glue decorations on to a cake using a piping bag and royal icing.

To fill a piping bag with no mess, put the bag inside a tall glass or a jug, fold the top of the bag over the rim, then fill.

Piping is easier if the cake is raised. If you don't have a turntable, place the cake on an inverted cake tin.

Keep your cake steady for decorating by making 4 equal-sized marzipan balls. Stand the cake on the marzipan balls and press down gently.

Soak a tea towel with water to place over royal icing to stop it from drying out and going hard.

For a neat finish, make sure you cover and edge your cake board.

Left-over royal icing? Just add a little more icing sugar and a few drops of peppermint essence, then roll out and cut into shapes to make peppermint creams.

To prevent breaking the icing when cutting a cake, dip the knife blade in boiling water first.

Other icings

You can keep buttercream for 2 or 3 weeks in a covered container in the fridge, so save time by making more than you need and add flavours to suit each cake you make.

Don't be scared of fondant icing – it's really just like using plasticine. If what you're doing goes horribly wrong, just squidge it back together and start again.

Always plan well in advance if you are

making any pastillage models or flowers, to allow for items to dry out properly.

Make sure cutters are completely dry after washing, or they'll go rusty and you'll have to throw them away. The best way is to place them in the oven as it's cooling down after a baking session.

If you're rolling out coloured fondant icing, don't dust the board with icing sugar – it makes the colour paler. Instead, rub good old Trex (or similar) over the rolling surface and put the icing directly on that. It never sticks.

Fondant icing is best worked at room temperature. Don't even attempt to roll it straight from the fridge – it will crack.

Store fondant icing in thin polythene bags or wrap carefully in cling film. The important thing is to exclude air or it will dry out, so squeeze out as much as you can from the bag before storing in the fridge.

Use a small spirit level to make sure the dowelling is even on fondant-covered tiered cakes.

For adding tiny amounts of food colouring and flavouring, use an eye-dropper bought from the chemist.

To avoid streaks when adding paste colour to fondant icing, add the colour to a small quantity of icing first, then blend that into the rest of the icing, otherwise you'll be plagued with streaks.

To colour fondant icing really evenly takes ages. Give yourself plenty of time or, alternatively, decide on a marbled effect and make a virtue of the streaks!

Sponge cakes

Jam spreads more easily on a sponge cake if you warm it first.

For firmer whipped cream, beat it with honey rather than sugar.

For an extra-light sponge cake, beat a tablespoon of hot water into the mixture just before baking.

When dividing cake mix between 2 (or more) tins, weigh the tins before putting in the oven and even up the mixture as necessary.

Leftovers
Barry Jones; Elizabeth Orme; Fay Kingsley

Always make stock from the turkey bones. Simmer for a couple of hours with trimmings of leeks, leftover celery and leftover veg, then strain and freeze.

To make a fast and tasty dressing for turkey salad, mix chutney with mayonnaise or yoghurt and fold in the chopped cooked meat.

Bread rolls that have gone hard can be crumbed in the food processor with a few cloves of garlic. Freeze and use as a topping for pasta and vegetable bakes.

Left-over Stilton can be frozen, then used to stuff chicken breasts, or it can be melted into Stilton soup.

Grated parmesan rind can be stirred into soup for extra taste.

Leftover stuffing can be mixed with mince to make a tasty meat loaf.

Keep bits and bobs of leftover wine to add to sauces and casseroles.

Mince pies will keep in an airtight container for about 2 weeks. Alternatively they will freeze well.

The last scraps of Christmas pud can be broken up in a food processor and mixed into home-made ice cream.

Alternatively, fry leftover Christmas pud in butter next day.

Mix fruit-cake trimmings with brandy and mincemeat until nice and soft. Roll into balls and dip into chocolate vermicelli, or cover with icing for mini Christmas puds.

Festive Drink
Berry Bros. and Rudd (www.bbr.com); Avril Abbott

Wine

Remember when buying wine that between £1.80 and £2.00 of the retail price is accounted for by the cost of the bottle, the label, the cork, the capsule, VAT. It's worth forking out a bit more – you'll get a better bottle of wine.

When selecting a wine to drink with food, take into account the way the food is prepared and in particular any sauces that will be served.

Wines from the Gamay grape are fruity and fresh, and can do battle with cranberry sauce. Off-dry Riesling wines go well with turkey, as the hint of sweetness complements the meat. Otherwise spoil yourself with a good Pinot Noir.

Taking a cork out of a bottle of red wine only gets air into the very top of the bottle. If you wish to let the wine 'breathe', then it must be decanted into another vessel.

Red wine too young? Pass the wine from the bottle to the decanter and then back again (using a funnel) to get as much air into the wine as possible. This will prematurely age it and soften out the wine.

However, you can mask the poor quality of most wines by decanting it – which also means knowledgeable guests won't be able to read the label. But …

It is easy to destroy an old bottle of wine by decanting it. Too much air and the wine will be over the hill. Better instead to pour the wine carefully from bottle to glass so as not to disturb any sediment.

To remove a stubborn cork, dip a woollen cloth into boiling water and wrap tightly round the bottle neck. This will loosen the cork.

Don't scrimp with a good meal by using plonk to make a sauce. The better the wine, the better the sauce. However, a full-bodied red is preferable over a watery one.

Your guests shouldn't be guinea pigs: a dinner party is not the best time to try out an exciting new wine from Estonia that you found at the off-licence. Test it out on your own first. A bottle of acid rain will ruin the party.

The larger the bottle, the longer the wine will keep, and the more slowly it will mature, owing to the fact that there is less surface area of wine in contact with the air in the bottle.

'A glass of wine without some cheese is like a kiss without a squeeze.'

The words 'fine champagne' on a bottle of cognac refer to a blend of wines from two of the authorised cognac wine-making areas, Grande Champagne and Petite Champagne.

Stick a silver spoon into the neck of a champagne bottle to stop the contents going flat. It will stay fizzy for about a day.

Liven up festive champagne by dropping a few whole raspberries and halved straw-berries into a champagne flute. Pour in

1 tablespoon crème de framboise and 2 tablespoons vodka. Top up with chilled
champagne.

**Alternatively, mix together 5 tablespoons
chopped fresh mint**, 3 tablespoons lime
juice and 3 tablespoons caster sugar in a large
jug. Stir well and top up with champagne.
Pour into tall glasses over ice and top with a
sprig of mint.

Champagne should be stored between
12°C and 18°C, and should be chilled, ready
to serve, at 7°C.

The colder the champagne, the less likely
it is to explode when you take out the cork.

**The more slowly you remove a cham-
pagne cork**, the less of an explosion it will
create. Take off the wire and hold the bottle
with one hand, twisting off the cork. As you
feel it releasing, try to hold it on and gently
release it.

Open champagne without fuss by clamp-
ing the cork with a pair of nutcrackers and
gently turning the bottle, *not* the cork.

When making mulled wine, let the
mixture stand for 5–10 minutes to let the
flavours infuse.

**Keep wines and ports lying on their sides
but spirits standing upright.** The high percentage of alcohol (40 per cent) in spirits can
corrode the metal caps. Champagnes can be
stored lying down or standing up, as the

extra-wide cork ensures a very tight seal.

Try to store your wine somewhere cool (8–13ºC). An absence of light, heat and vibration makes for the best environment of all.

A good way to make a half-opened bottle of wine last longer is to decant it into a smaller bottle, thus reducing the amount of wine exposed to oxygen.

If you want the best from either vintage port or fino/amontillado sherry, you should not keep them, once opened, for more than a week, although tawny ports will last a bit longer.

If the weather is bitter, or one of your house guests has a cold, mix up a traditional hot toddy with 300ml (half a pint) boiling water, 8 teaspoons runny honey, 4 teaspoons lemon juice and 4 shots whisky. Divide between 4 heatproof glasses and stir well.

Cocktails
Ed Barnes; Jamie Francis; Jack Harrison

IN THE SPIRIT

To be properly chilled, a glass should be placed in the fridge at least a couple of hours before serving. If you have forgotten to do this, simply fill the glass with ice, swish it around and then empty it before pouring.

To frost a glass, put it in the freezer until a white frosted look appears. Alternatively, bury it in ice cubes until the same thing happens.

Handle glasses by the stem – you don't want to warm the glass after you've chilled it or leave fingerprints.

For drinks that call for a sugar frosting, take the frosted glass and wipe the rim with a slice of lemon or lime. Then dip in powdered sugar to complete the effect.

Margaritas are prepared in the same way, but the rim is coated with lime and dipped in coarse salt. Don't get the glasses mixed up!

If you're making cocktails at home, don't buy an expensive ice crusher; just wrap the ice in a clean tea towel and smash it up with a meat mallet or even an ordinary hammer.

Never scoop up ice for a cocktail using the glass itself – it may break! If this happens, throw away the ice immediately. You don't want to drink ground glass.

No need to stir a drink that contains a car-bonated mixer; it does most of its own mixing naturally by bubbling. If you think it needs a helping hand, give it 2 stirs – but no more.

When making highballs, make sure the glass is two thirds full of ice before adding spirits. For lowballs, fill the glass about half full of ice before pouring the drink.

Ice makes whisky too cold and reduces its flavour.

Don't use soda in whisky – it ruins the taste.

Whisky evaporates very quickly, so keep the cap tightly screwed on.

Always keep a few chillies marinated in sherry to add a kick to a Bloody Mary.

Be very careful not to keep the ice in a shaker longer than the time it takes to chill the ingredients. The ice will begin to melt and you will be left with a watered-down cocktail.

Remember, a 'dash' means 4 or 5 drops.

Never use the best-quality alcohol for cocktails. The less expensive ones work just as well when they are mixed with juices, carbonated drinks, etc.

When mixing the different ingredients, add the cheaper ones first, so that expensive ingredients don't get wasted in the event of a mistake.

A good present idea for a keen cocktail drinker would be a hamper, with olives, lemons, swizzle stick and a couple of highball glasses. Add miniature bottles of spirits too. Wrap the contents in a pretty basket or ice bucket – with a ribbon, of course.

When inventing your own cocktails, try to balance the flavours in the drink by combining something sweet (such as fruit liqueur) with something sharp or bitter (such as lemon juice). Most classic cocktails achieve this balance.

Rinse your shot glasses frequently. Spirits can taint each other or cloud your drink.

Try to avoid using plastic cocktail sticks as they tend to give a cocktail a slightly artificial appearance.

In fruit drinks, such as strawberry margaritas, always use fresh fruit, not frozen.

Most shaken drinks that contain single cream can also be made as blended drinks, substituting vanilla ice cream for the single cream – a kind of alcoholic smoothie!

Shake any drinks made with juices, sugar, eggs, or cream, or use an electric blender.

Improvise a cocktail shaker using a long and a short glass, held together at the join.

LAYERS AND LAYERS

A useful tip when layering a drink: if you don't know the specific gravity of a liqueur, read and compare the proofs on the bottle. Liqueurs with lower proofs generally contain more sugar and are thicker and heavier.

Remember: the same type of flavoured liqueurs, when made by different companies, can sometimes have different proofs (or specific gravities). This may conflict with the other liqueurs and spoil the layered presentation.

When layering drinks, rest a spoon against the inside of the glass and pour the liqueur over the back or rounded side of the spoon. The liqueur should run down the inside of the glass and rest on top of the drink.

Use the same technique when pouring cream on to Irish coffee.

If the glass is too narrow to place a spoon in, trickle the liqueur over a maraschino cherry.

If you mess up the layers, place the drink in the fridge for about 1 hour and the liqueurs will separate themselves.

If you find cocktails often leave you with a nasty hangover, try drinking cocktails with fresh fruit juice in them. The juice will replace the vitamins that your body loses through drinking, and the fructose will help absorb the alcohol.

PACK A PUNCH

The best way to keep party punch cool is to freeze some of the punch in ice-cube trays or a ring mould. Float the frozen punch in your bowl to keep it chilled but undiluted.

To decorate punch for a special occasion, core and slice apples, and use pastry cutters or a sharp knife to cut out shapes. Dip in lemon juice and float on the punch.

Treat adult party guests to jelly made with a large dash of vodka or champagne. Enjoy experimenting with quantities at home.

For very special party nibbles, inject cherry tomatoes with vodka and Worcestershire sauce. Sprinkle with celery salt and black pepper for a very original take on the traditional Bloody Mary.

Store fresh ginger in vodka – it will improve the taste of the vodka *and* the ginger.

Flavoured vodka is all the rage in pubs and clubs, so try making your own – cordials or crushed and puréed fruit can be added. Experiment with lighter and heavier cordials than the vodka itself for a pretty, layered drink.

GETTING FRUITY

Lemons and oranges give more juice if soaked first in warm water.

When you refrigerate cut fruit, cover it with a damp napkin. This will help to keep the juices in.

Orange slices should be cut about 5mm (a quarter of an inch) thick. Thicker slices are not economical and waste orange; thinner slices will be too flimsy.

When cutting fruit, slice in half from tip to tip, then slit the flesh down the middle without slicing through the rind. Then turn the fruit flesh-side down and slice. This leaves a slit in the middle of the wedge to hang on the glass.

To cut 'twists', slice the ends of a lemon just

to the flesh. Then cut slits lengthwise through the rind, but not quite down to the flesh. Continue slicing around the lemon with 5mm (quarter-inch) gaps. Then you can peel the twists off the lemon.

When using a twist, rub the top of the glass with the rind side (which contains more aromatic oil), then actually twist it and place it in the drink.

You should be able to get about 16 wedges per lime.

When squeezing a wedge of lime, shield it with your hand to prevent lime juice from squirting your guests in the eye – very painful!

When you slice a lemon for your G&T, rather than letting the rest dry out, slice it up and freeze in water in an ice-cube tray for next time.

Freeze cranberries, chopped fruit or herbs into ice cubes to liven up cocktails. *Make sure it's nothing poisonous.*

UP IN FLAMES

It is always easier to flame brandy, or other high-alcohol spirits, by warming the glass first. You can do this by holding the glass by its stem above the flame or electric coil of your stove until it feels warm. Avoid touching the glass to the flame or coil, as this can char or crack the glass.

It may sound obvious, but keep your head away from the cocktail glass when flaming spirits! Many an eyebrow has been lost this way ...

An impressive trick: light a glass with a little Sambuca in it, put your hand over the glass to extinguish the flame, and when the flame goes out, the decrease in air temperature creates a strong suction on your hand – strong enough that you can shake your hand all around without the glass coming off.

THE MORNING AFTER

A prairie oyster is an ideal hangover cure. Rinse a glass with olive oil. Add tomato ketchup and a whole egg yolk. Season with Worcestershire sauce, vinegar, salt and pepper. Swallow the mixture in one gulp.

When cleaning ashtrays after a long night, try using soda water. The bubbles will help to shift the ash, so you don't have to wipe them.

Cheat's Christmas

Cheat's Kitchen
Deirdre Finlay; Harry Snape; Gillian Fitzgerald

Buy a ready-made pud and inject some brandy.

Buy jars of supermarket mincemeat and add a few of your own ingredients – cherries, nuts, brandy – to make it more luxurious.

Many supermarkets sell undecorated

Christmas cakes. Simply ice and decorate it yourself, or buy an iced cake and remove the tacky decorations. Make it look home-made with holly, pine cones, ribbon or simple cinnamon sticks, bound with raffia or ribbon and laid on the top.

Gently lift the top off shop-bought mince pies and replace with stars cut out of marzipan or fondant icing.

Jazz up shop-bought mince pies by lifting off the lid before warming and putting in a small amount of brandy butter. It will melt as you warm the mince pie and make it taste creamy and special.

Dried chestnuts are available all year round in health food stores and Italian delis, so you can buy them well in advance. No boiling or peeling involved – just soak in cold water overnight, then use as in the recipe.

Ready-prepared chestnuts in tins are on sale at Christmas time. They are expensive but if time and not money is short, they're ideal.

Slash the time it takes to make giblet stock by using the microwave. Place thawed giblets in a microwaveable bowl with 1 large onion, roughly chopped, 6 black peppercorns, a pinch of salt and about 1 pint of boiling water. Cover tightly and cook on high for 10–12 minutes. Use immediately or strain and refrigerate for up to 24 hours.

Soften butter fast in the microwave when

making brandy butter. Remove the wrapper, place on a plate and give it 20-second bursts on defrost until it is malleable. Be careful, because it tends to soften fastest in the middle.

Make microwave croutons, using small cubes of bread cut from a white or brown loaf. Spread over the base of a large dish or plate and cook on high for 3–4 minutes.

Ripen green bananas for trifle by heating in the microwave on high for about 1 minute.

Make custard in double-quick time in the microwave. Give it short bursts of cooking (1 minute 30 seconds, then 1 minute, then 30 seconds as it thickens), and keep whisking with a balloon whisk in between and any lumps will be bashed to pieces.

Take the labels off interesting jams or chutneys, replace with handwritten labels and decorate with a ribbon.

If you run out of full or semi-skimmed milk, use skimmed and add a knob of butter.

Short of space to warm plates and serving dishes? Put them in the dishwasher, and when the cycle has finished, they will be good and warm.

Cheating Around the House

Avoid the embarrassment of having to undo the top button of your trousers or skirt when you have overdone it at Christmas dinner. Thread an elastic band through the buttonhole and around the button. Plenty of room then for expansion!

Tart up old decorations and baubles with a can of metallic spray paint.

Fill out a sparse Christmas tree with fake foliage. Add a few drops of pine oil, and no one will know the difference.

You can improve on cheap crackers by slipping in better presents, but you will have to open them up with care.

Home-made Christmas

Home Baking
Mary Neal, Sally Love

Make your own candied peel – much cheaper and better than the shop kind. Scrub lemons, oranges and limes clean with water and a dash of vinegar; rinse and dry. Quarter the fruits and remove the peel, then cut into strips. Simmer the peel for about 2 hours, checking regularly to keep the water topped up just to cover. Stir in 1 heaped tablespoon of sugar for each whole fruit and bring to the boil, then switch off the heat and allow to stand overnight. Simmer for about 5 minutes on each of the next 2 days, then drain and dry in a very low oven for about 12 hours. Keep in a cool place, loosely wrapped in foil or silicon paper.

Make scented sugars for baking or as Christmas gifts. Try a vanilla pod, a combination of cinnamon, some cloves and a nutmeg, some dried lavender flowers, scented geranium leaves or dried citrus rind.

Make fabulous spiced nuts in minutes – ideal for cocktail parties or as gifts. Heat a little oil in a microwaveable dish on high power for 2 minutes, then add 1 teaspoon each of salt, celery seasoning and chilli powder. Stir and cook on high for 1 minute, then stir in about 350g (12oz) mixed nuts (almonds are best). Cook on high for about 5 minutes, stirring occasionally.

Presents
Patricia Kirkpatrick; Sally Mavers; Jane Purchon; Cecily Gotram

Put together a hamper – treats for the person who has everything and essentials for an elderly person who lives alone. Hampers can be tailor-made to suit the recipient: gardening implements, seeds, gardeners' skin care and so on for the green-fingered; scented candles, soaps, essential oils for the fan of alternative therapies. Cooks might like special preserves and chutneys, quirky cooking utensils and a newly published cookery book. Make a pillow in the bottom with tissue paper, pile in the gifts, cover the hamper with cling film and attach a large ribbon.

A thoughtful present for the recipient to enjoy months later is to plant up a galvanised metal or terracotta pot with bulbs. Daffodils (delicious-smelling Tête-à-Tête perhaps) will need to be put in compost in September, but tulips can wait until November.

Plan well in advance and plant up forced hyacinths that will bloom around Christmas. Tie a matching ribbon around the pot.

For proud grandparents, mount a drawing by one of your children on gingham paper or fabric, glue with spray mount to a stiff piece of card and frame.

Create your own picture too for grand-parents: have your children make an impression of their hands with paint or in plaster, and frame the result with dates and names.

Customise a plain photograph frame by gluing on buttons and beads, shells, pebbles and glass beads, or dried flowers. You can seal the decoration with varnish.

Create a memory of the year or a special holiday by mounting mementoes (shells, pebbles, feathers, photographs) stuck down with a glue gun and presented in a box frame.

Buy three small pots of herbs (basil, chives, etc. are available from supermarkets) and surround them with tissue paper inside a small round basket.

Home-made chocolates or truffles, packed in tissue in a small paper gift box, make a simple present.

Christmas stockings can be an expensive rip-off. Bundle up presents in a pillowcase, or use a pretty tablecloth or piece of velvet fabric and tie it to the end of the bed *à la* Dick Whittington.

Alternatively, fill a wellie.

Present jars or bottles in simple paper bags with handles and tie the handles with polka-dot bows. Perhaps they could be the ingredients to someone's favourite recipe.

Wrapping

Part of the pleasure of presents is in the wrapping. Use Japanese paper or sparkly tissue paper. Add a fan of coordinating, con-certinaed paper and glue it to the top.

Thread ribbon through contrasting buttons and glue the ribbon on the back, or glue on little batches of sparkly sequins.

For a really special present, wrap it with ribbon and insert lavender stalks or a couple of rosebuds under the bow.

Paint some white paper with black foun-tain-pen ink, and when it has dried, draw patterns with a paintbrush dipped in house-hold bleach. The effect is wonderful.

Use a rubber stamp, or even a potato with a shape cut out, dipped into paint, to make your own wrapping paper. Print on to plain paper.

Use old sheets of music as wrapping paper. You can 'age' it by rubbing it with a tea bag dipped in water, then leave it to dry.

Use layers of different-coloured tissue paper for a cheap and effective way to wrap a gift. Gather the paper around the top and secure with ribbon, then fluff out the paper.

Wrap a present in offcuts of fabric in the same way.

Stop sharp corners of boxes from tearing wrapping paper by attaching a small piece of sticky tape to the inside of the paper at each corner to reinforce it.

Double-sided sticky tape gives a really professional finish.

To remove the sticky residue left by labels from a present, simply dip a cotton bud into some methylated spirit, rub it over the sticky patch and leave for about 15 minutes, then rub off.

To wrap a tie, fold it once, then attach with 2 rubber bands to a piece of card. It will keep flat this way.

Save money on present tags (and save them parting company with the present). Buy plain white parcel stickers (available from stationers) and decorate with an edging line using a gold pen, or a simple holly-leaf motif. Stamp too with a festive stamp, usually available from stationers.

Alternatively, cut out squares or triangles of the same wrapping paper and stick on to white card to use as present tags.

Wrap presents in brown parcel paper or wallpaper lining paper and brighten up with jewel-coloured ribbon.

Fold the wrapping paper into two folds (as if you were making a fan), then wrap the present for a lovely effect.

For children, attach a raffle-ticket number to their present, then give them the corresponding number. They then have to find the present that matches it.

Keep a couple of extra presents (some for children, some for adults) in case someone drops in and gives you a present unexpectedly.

Crackers
Mary Neal, Sally Love

Make your own French crackers: lay out a sheet of coloured tissue paper, place a small present inside (nail varnish, lipstick, earrings, cufflinks, chocolates, small toys), gather up the corners of the tissue paper and tie in a bow with coloured net.

Drizzle some confetti into home-made crackers for a shower when they are pulled.

Fill your own crackers with joke-shop novelties.

Decorating the Home

Trees

Robert Matthews, Chesham; David Thompson, The Christmas Shop

Choosing your tree

The commonest tree you will find is the Norway spruce. Other trees have distinctive characteristics:

- **Nordmanniana:** the Nordmann or Caucasian fir has glossy deep-green needles that are soft to the touch, grow right round the branches and hold well to the tree.
- **Scots Pine:** its strong but rather upright branches retain their long needles well, and the colour ranges from dark to bright green with some trees being bluish tinged.
- **Blue Spruce:** one of the most attractive of all the Christmas trees, but the short and quite sharp needles are dusty-blue in colour. It must be freshly cut and well watered to retain its needles.
- **Omorika:** also known as the Serbian spruce. The blue-green needles are flat and slightly curved. It must be kept well watered to prevent needle drop.
- **Noble Fir:** an increasingly popular choice for Christmas trees, and its foliage is often used for wreaths and garlands. The needles are a silvery bluish-green, and stay on the tree well.

Give the tree a shake when you are choosing one, and make sure there are no falling needles. It's the sure sign of an old tree.

Run your hand gently along a branch in the opposite direction to the lie of the needles. On a fresh tree, the needles will stay put.

Look at the tree outside of its net and make sure there are no dull needles. Shiny needles are best.

Fresh trees will be full of sap and very heavy. A light tree is dried out and old, so leave it well alone.

Always look out for a tree with a nice dark-green colour. Avoid anything yellowish.

If possible, go to a plantation where you can choose your tree and see it cut there and then.

Work out the right height for your tree, then take someone along of the same height or thereabouts. Tall husbands come in very handy for this.

If the Christmas trees are in a windy, sunny or exposed area, they can dry out fast and the needles will fall earlier. Choose a tree from a sheltered place.

Check the smell of the needles before you choose your tree. Some types are actually unpleasant, some don't have much scent at all, but others are lovely.

Buy a rootballed or a container-grown tree and after Twelfth Night, plant it outside, near enough to the house that you can deck it with lights next year.

Tree care

Don't bring your tree into the house too soon – no more than 2 weeks prior to Christmas. Keep it outside in water until you're ready to decorate it.

If your tree is wrapped in net, undo it straight away so that the branches have a chance to drop back to their natural position.

If you have to cut any of the branches off your tree, watch out for the resin that can ooze out. It will stain clothes and furniture.

Treat your Christmas tree like a bunch of flowers. Cut a small slice off the butt and stand it in a container full of water, secured with stones and scrunched-up newspaper. Water daily. A tree can drink up to 20fl oz (1 pint) of water a day.

Support the tree with bricks placed in the container, then use a piece of gutter piping to pour water into the container.

Keep trees away from radiators and fires.

If you have a dog or cat, hoover up the fallen needles regularly as they can get stuck in their paws and hurt them.

When getting a tree out of the house, wrap it in a sheet as if it was in a hammock, to avoid leaving a trail of needles.

Recycling trees: some local authorities have a recycling system for Christmas trees, which is usually available at the local household waste site. Alternatively you could hire a shredder (get everyone in your street to chip in on the hire price) and shred the trees. Use the chippings on the compost heap.

Decorating your tree

Trees with dense branches look best with wrap-round decorations, like tinsel and other garlands. Hanging decorations look better on a more open tree.

You can stand up a Christmas tree in a bucket of golf balls. Just make sure no one wants to play golf.

Try out your Christmas lights before you put them on the tree.

Put the lights on the tree first, wrapping them close to the trunk. Put the baubles on next, then the tinsel and finally the bows.

Make a small tree seem much larger by putting it on top of a trunk or a table, to give it height. Drape a floor-length tablecloth over the table before situating the tree, then use the remaining area of the tabletop to set out gifts. Surround the floor around the tree-laden table with various sizes and shapes of attractive baskets, prop open an antique trunk, or display a doll's pushchair. (An antique wicker cot placed near the tree can also be part of the Christmas decorations.)

For a rustic, traditional effect, drape an old quilt – not a valuable one – around the base of your tree instead of using a tree skirt. Or use tablecloths, bedcovers, and curtains that have irreparable damage or stains on them. Just pleat the cloth to hide the damaged areas as you wind it around the base of your tree. You can even use a very ruffled, layered, vintage petticoat as a tree support cover.

Instead of forcing a small loop of string over a branch to hang a decoration, simply open up a paper clip, slip the loop through the decoration and the other end over the branch.

Wrap your tree lights around a piece of cardboard so you aren't faced with spaghetti next year.

Save up egg boxes to store delicate bauble decorations.

Moulded polystyrene or cardboard trays for storing fruit in supermarkets are ideal for keeping larger delicate baubles safe. Just ask for them – they'll be thrown away otherwise.

No room for a tree? Buy hazel twigs from your florist, stand them in a good-sized urn and decorate with lights and decorations.

Alternatively hang a small Christmas tree from a curtain rail in a window.

Edible decorations

Children love these. To decorate your tree with Christmas biscuits, make them thin enough by rolling out the biscuit paste on the back of a baking tray. Cut out the biscuits but leave them in place. Remove the excess paste from between the shapes, and put the tray straight into the oven.

To make window biscuits, make up a short-bread biscuit mixture and roll out to about 5mm (a quarter-inch) thick. Cut out a large heart (or any other shape) using a biscuit cutter, then cut a smaller shape out of the middle. Place on a baking sheet lined with baking parchment. Crush coloured boiled sweets with a rolling pin and use to fill the smaller shape in the middle. Pierce the top of the biscuit with a skewer. Bake until golden brown. Leave to cool. When cold, thread ribbon through the hole and hang the biscuits on the tree or at a window …

… If the threading hole closes up during baking, make it again when the biscuits have just come out of the oven and are still soft.

Decorate a tree with whole lemons or oranges for a zesty festive aroma. Cinnamon bundles and spicy ginger biscuits add smell too (if the latter last long enough before they are eaten).

Around the House

Pick holly in mid to late November or early December, while the berries are still ripe. Put the stems into a bucket of damp sand and cover the top of the holly with a cloth. This keeps it fresh and prevents it from frost damage. *Remember: only cut holly from a permitted source, not from a hedgerow.*

Jazz up your holly by giving it a lovely frosted effect. First, wash it thoroughly in water. Allow to dry naturally, then dip it in melted margarine or lard and sprinkle all over with caster sugar. Allow to dry.

If you are hanging Christmas cards from ribbon or garlands, drill thin holes in the wall and insert little screw plugs. At Christmas time, screw in small cup hooks and attach the ribbon or twine to these.

Twist streamers by attaching them with a bulldog clip to the end of an electric screwdriver.

Hang sparkly decorations from the light fittings using fishing line – they will twinkle in the light as they rotate.

Jazz up plain baubles with braid and tassels from haberdashery shops. Stick on using a glue gun.

For a funky tree-top star or garland, straighten out a wire coat-hanger and bend it into shape. Then wind decorative beads threaded on to florists' wire all the way round and wire it to the tree.

Decorate windows with snowflake papercuts in festive colours – no need to stick to white. Fold a large sheet of paper many times and cut out small sections into shapes. Open out the paper for a symmetrical shape.

Make fake snow by adding a good handful of soapflakes to a little water and beat using an electric mixer. Apply it to trees (indoor), windows and garlands for a good and long-lasting effect.

A child's chair, or attractive doll furniture, placed near the Christmas tree, with a doll or teddy bear nestled in it (and dressed for Christmas), is another whimsical touch that allows a little to seem like more.

Ornaments are not only for your tree. Use them to spice up gift packages, to hang on doorknobs, as window-shade pulls, as place cards at a party. Alternatively, pile an old collection in a clear glass vase, or on a cake plate, to display as a centrepiece.

Crystal chandelier prisms, taken from dilapidated light fixtures that you can find at car boot sales and flea markets, make lovely additions to your Christmas tree, imparting the look of sparkling icicles. When the light catches the crystals, they cast tiny rainbows throughout the room.

Christmassy scents wafting though the house help a festive atmosphere. Spike an orange with cloves and boil with some cider. Or heat some cinnamon in a pan of boiling water, as if you were making tea.

Bring out Christmas CDs and keep the music playing throughout the season to bring happy sounds to every room in the house, even the bathroom. Put a couple of jingle bells in the cylindrical, plastic toilet-paper holder.

Make a fragrant fire with pine cones, orange peel, logs from apple or cedar trees, or prunings of bay, eucalyptus or cypress.

To make an inexpensive and cheerful window display, wrap miniature Christmas lights and garlands around a wreath or bell from a craft or art shop.

Adorn the house with attractive vintage books. Think of books as art objects and display them as you would your favourite collectibles. Wrap a group of three with attractive ribbon.

If they are of no further use as books (perhaps being damaged or outdated), spray the covers with gold, silver, or white spray paint and wrap with ribbon. Use these as a pedestal-type base on which to display flowers, baskets, ceramic figurines of angels and the like.

Spray two pineapples with gold paint, and place at either end of the mantelpiece for a strikingly effective display.

Dry slices of fruit in the oven or airing cupboard, spray with gold or silver paint and hang from the tree or in a wreath.

Wreaths and Door Decorations

An easy door decoration: flatten out a square of chicken wire, and use wire to attach holly or other greenery, baubles and ribbon to cover the whole square.

Cover a wire wreath frame with moss
(both available from florists) and use wire to
secure it tightly. Push wire through the centre
of the decorations that you want to use and
twist the two ends tightly together. Then
push the wire through the moss frame,
working from the inside of the wreath out
and filling any gaps.

Buy a wreath base from a florist and
attach holly, spruce and bright red apples
using florists' wire. The wreath should last
about 12 days hung outside. Simply replace
anything that wilts or wrinkles.

Other ideas for adding to wreaths:
oranges, pine cones, teasels, berries and
twigs, lavender, thistles, cinnamon sticks.
Include nuts like pecans, walnuts, almonds
and hazelnuts. Lay the wreath on newspaper,
spray the nuts with spray adhesive and cover
sections of them with gold leaf.

Roll chicken wire into baubles and spray
with gold paint, then add to a wreath.

**If you are using roses in a Christmas
wreath**, spray it regularly with water to keep
them fresh.

Before using pine cones to decorate,
place them on a baking sheet in a low oven
(about 120°C, 250°F, gas mark a quarter) for
about 1 hour. The heat will cause the cones to
'blossom' and open more fully. (And the scent
is enhanced as well – at least while they are
warm.)

Centrepieces and Table Decorations

Protect your table from spills by placing a layer of cling film over it before you put on the tablecloth.

An effective but simple idea for a table centre is to buy painted twigs from a florist (or spray-paint some yourself), then hang sweets wrapped in coloured Cellophane paper from the twigs. Add glass baubles too.

Miniature conifers in pots make terrific centrepieces. Wrap some thin ribbon in a spiral from top to bottom and pop pine cones, kumquats and tiny baubles round the base.

Bowls of fresh fruit and nuts – lemons, limes, oranges, pomegranates, apples, pecans, walnuts – are lovely Christmas statements. Place fruit in your most attractive bowls in strategic areas of your home, perhaps insert-ing a sprig of rosemary or pine as an embellishment. If your house doesn't get overly warm in winter, the fruit should last for at least 2 weeks. Be sure to choose only the freshest, unblemished fruits for this job – check them periodically and remove any moisture in the bottom of the bowls. When Christmas is over, use the fruit and nuts in baking and cooking.

Commercially freeze-dried or dehy-drated fruits are available as well. These are much lighter in weight than fresh fruit (and are not edible), and may be reused for several years; however, they are much more expensive. Alternatively, you can slice and dry apples, oranges, and other citrus fruits. These are lovely as tree ornaments or can enhance a home-made pot-pourri.

Leaves from most citrus and eucalyptus trees are very fragrant at this time of year. These types of leaves hold up quite well, looking fine even after several weeks.

Score firm limes into sections using a sharp knife, and dry them in a low oven (about 120°C, 250°F, gas mark a quarter). Store them in a cool bag for a couple of days with some tangy citrus oil, and hang them, threaded with wire and topped with ribbon, on the tree or along a mantelpiece.

Score a lime with a grooved blade (available from art shops), making interesting patterns, and paint the scored lines with lemon or lime juice to stop them going brown. Insert cloves into the lines for added interest.

Roll interesting-shaped fruits (pears, plums, figs or kumquats) in beaten egg white, then coat in a mixture of granulated and caster sugar. Leave to dry thoroughly before arranging as a table centre.

You can create a striking centrepiece for a table by filling a terracotta urn with sand and inserting long taper candles into it at angles. Cover the top of the sand with damp moss. *Never leave lit candles unattended.*

No tablecloth big enough? Use a king-sized white sheet – it is easy to wash afterwards if wine is spilt.

For a simple table centre, float small candles in a glass bowl of water.

Bring Christmas roses in from the garden to decorate the table, but make sure they get lots of water by pricking the stems several times below the water line. Make them last longer by dipping the stems in boiling water, leaving them overnight up to their necks in cold water, and putting them in a vase with plenty of fresh water.

Fill a glass bowl with shiny satsumas for a simple (and edible) centrepiece.

For a truly festive aroma, stud a bowlful of oranges with cloves.

Create a wintry smell with a pot-pourri made from cinnamon, lavender, orange and lime.

For place names, write each guest's name in gold metallic pen on a large holly leaf.

Or write each guest's name in sparkly nail varnish on their glass. You can remove it with nail varnish remover later.

Tie gold, red or green ribbon on to the back of chairs.

Wrap ivy around crisp table napkins.

Shine your silver cutlery and candlesticks

until they sparkle by placing a plate-sized piece of aluminium foil into a bowl with 1 tablespoon of salt to 10fl oz (half a pint) of water. Drop the silver in and leave for 1–2 minutes. Rinse and dry it, wearing gloves to avoid leaving finger marks.

As an alternative, try putting 1 tablespoon of whiting (available at hardware stores) into a small bowl. Mix it to a cream with water, then add 1–2 drops of household ammonia or meths. Wipe the mixture on to the silver and off again, rinse the cutlery and finish with a chamois leather.

Wrap your silver cutlery until the next special occasion in dark tissue paper and a plastic bag, squeezing out as much air as possible.

Most people don't have a different set of dishes for Christmas, but you can get the same effect if you buy clear glass dishes and set them on top of paper plates with a Christmassy design. A 25cm (10-inch) paper plate fits perfectly under a dinner plate, and 15cm (6-inch) paper plates will go under a soup bowl or salad plate.

Under a lace tablecloth, use a paper cloth, a coloured sheet, or an inexpensive piece of fabric for a colour-coordinated scheme.

Make informal Christmas place mats (or get the kids to make them) by recycling last year's Christmas cards. Cut out the design elements you like, and sandwich them between 2 pieces of clear contact paper.

Lights and Candles

You can prolong the burning time of a candle by putting it in the fridge for a day before lighting.

Use a collection of old kilner jars, especially tinted ones, filled with sand (about a quarter to a third full depending upon the size of your candle and jar) in which you have placed a night-light candle, to embellish the festive mood. Place this collection on your windowsill, on the mantelpiece, or in the centre of your table. Leave the lid off (perhaps propped against the side of the jar) and enjoy the glow of candlelight.

Or combine tinted and/or clear kilner jars (perhaps in graduating sizes) and loosely fill them with a curled strand of tiny white Christmas lights (electric or battery operated). Decorate the rims of select jars with raffia, or tulle bows.

For a different effect, freeze water in different-size cartons, arrange in a dish, and put night-light candles of varying sizes in the midst of the ice blocks.

Support candles by sitting them in a glass bowl or dish, surrounded either by glass beads or by pebbles that have been spray painted gold and silver.

Terracotta plant pots can be painted or left plain. Fill with oasis, push the candle into the oasis and surround the candle with pebbles (as above), nuts or satsumas.

On the mantelpiece or on the table, use wine glasses of different designs and heights (you can pick them up at flea markets), and put coloured votive candles in them. You can add a small wreath or pine cones around the base.

Stand any candle arrangement on top of a mirror; it will glow even more brightly.

Candles create atmosphere immediately. Use scented candles and they can change the atmosphere of a room. Place candles in front of a mirror and they will reflect the light.

Line a mantelpiece with a row of tiny gold candles or night lights.

Making your own candles

Remember to keep candles away from decorations or fabrics and never leave lit candles unattended.

You will need a wick holder, wire core wicks, 200g (7oz) wax for 4–8 medium-sized tumblers, melted with microcrystalline soft wax (beaded wax pellets). Anchor the wick to the bottom of the container using the wick holder, and pour in 2cm (three quarters of an inch) of molten wax. Allow the wax to harden. Tie the wick to a wooden skewer resting across the top of the container. Fill the container with more wax and leave to cool. Top up as necessary with more wax. Remove the skewer and trim the wick to about 1cm (half an inch) from the top of the wax.

When melting your wax, avoid overheating it by placing it in a metal bowl over a saucepan of water.

If the wax catches fire, smother the flames with a damp cloth or a saucepan lid. Never douse with water.

Make sure the wick is straight and dry.

The wick size must be equal to the diameter of the candle; for example, a 25mm (1in) visible wick is suitable for a 25mm (1in) diameter candle.

Make sure the wick is not too thick or it will soot and smoke.

Keep the wick at around 1cm (half an inch) before lighting the candle.

One sheet of beeswax to 2kg (4lb) of wax will be enough to give wax a warm colour.

Always leave a newly made candle 24 hours before lighting it.

To make a simple candle, use old jelly moulds or pretty glass dishes, tumblers or footed dishes.

To make a square candle, cut off the bottom of an empty square juice carton and use as a mould to make your candle. Once it has set, carefully tear away the carton.

Parties

Dinner, Dance and Cocktail Parties

Elegant Days, Warwick and London

At a dinner party, a good host and hostess will move to another place after each course so that they can give each guest their attention. A move to the sitting room for pudding, coffee and brandy can help shake up the party.

The perfect number to have for a dinner party is 8.

A good host never runs short of drinks or food. Buy too much rather than risk running out.

Entertain 20 people well rather than 30 badly.

It's a good idea to invite the neighbours to a potentially noisy party. That way they can't complain!

Turn down the central heating a couple of notches before your guests arrive. People create their own heat.

Keep the party room more humid by placing a bowl or glass of water next to a radiator. Adding a couple of drops of perfume will create a pleasant smell too.

Put decorations right in the middle of

plate-glass windows so that tipsy guests don't walk into them.

Leave disposable cameras on the table(s), so guests can snap the people around them and you will have a record of the event.

Make sure you buy plenty of blank video-tapes and make sure you know how to programme the video before you go out to parties or invite guests in. If you can't be bothered to label what you've taped, cut out the entry from the newspaper and stick it to the outside of the box.

Get your guests in the party mood: blow up loads of balloons and scatter them all over the dance floor.

Put balloons in the tumble-dryer for a couple of minutes. They'll be much easier to blow up.

Try local catering colleges for waiters for your party. They'll be cheap, keen and very efficient.

Save on washing up after a party – buy disposable paper cups and customise with cut-out paper snowflakes.

Reduce condensation on your windows from all those heavy-breathing guests. A dish of salt on the windowsill will absorb a lot of the moisture.

A bowl of cider vinegar placed behind the

curtains will help clear the smell of cigarette smoke.

Put food and drink in different areas, so that your guests will be sure to circulate.

Party Food

Keep salad leaves in iced water before serving to stop them wilting. Drain and shake off excess water just before serving.

Winter barbecues are great fun, provided the weather is mild and everyone is wrapped up warmly. Coffee in a thermos and mince pies will create a festive atmosphere.

To avoid running out of fridge space during Christmas, invest in a couple of cool boxes, add a bag of ice or ice packs and use to store your party nibbles.

To make life easier for yourself, make sure you have a mixture of cold and hot canapés, and serve the cold ones first while the others are warming through.

To get neat, even-sized canapés (bread for crostini, or when making smoked salmon or ham pinwheels, for example), freeze, and cut the bread before it is completely defrosted.

As a rough guide:
- *For 10–20 people:* 4 cold savoury choices, 2 hot savoury choices, 8–12 canapés each.
- *For 30–40 people:* 5 cold savoury choices, 3 hot savoury choices, 8–12 canapés each.

- **_For 50–60 people:_** 4 cold savoury choices, 3 hot savoury choices, 1 cold sweet, 8–12 canapés each.

Salty snacks make guests more thirsty. And then they'll get drunker!

Party Drink

You won't get tiddly too fast if you drink a big glass of milk and have a piece of bread before you party.

Store cans of beer and bottles of water in a bath of cold water and ice – or on cold nights simply leave them outside the back door.

To stop your fizzy drinks overflowing, make sure the glasses are warm, then add ice to chill them.

Champagne in danger of overflowing? Dip your finger into the bubbles and you'll save the day.

Cool wine down more quickly by removing the cork first.

Chill the glasses for beer rather than the beer itself, otherwise the flavour can change a bit.

Add a good sprinkle of salt to the ice in your ice bucket – it cools down the wine much faster.

For hangovers, try tonic water at breakfast the morning after.

Children's Parties

Have a Santa's Sack full of little presents instead of playing pass-the-parcel. When the music stops, the first child to sit down can rummage for a present in Santa's Sack.

Plan children's parties so that they will be eating at the usual time. Really hungry kids won't enjoy themselves.

Make sure any running around games are played before the children eat – you don't want them all throwing up during musical chairs.

Make sure every child wins a little prize – they can get upset if they feel left out.

If there is going to be an entertainer, such as a clown or magician, make sure the children get a good look at him or her while their parents are still there. If they feel a bit nervous at first, their parents can reassure them.

Office Parties

Spend the early part of the evening impressing bosses and clients – you can get round to drinking later when they've all left.

Make sure you aren't handed your P45 on

Monday morning by staying sober. Drink plenty of milk and eat bread before you go.

At parties where clients or customers are invited, give everyone a name tag so that everyone knows who everyone else is.

At small office events, appoint a barperson, so that there isn't a free-for-all with the drinks.

If you're in charge, choose a venue, especially a themed one, because at a hotel there is little else to do other than drink.

The more people have to do, the better. A dinner dance with food and drink is a recipe for a drunken brawl. Provide games, fun fairs, entertainers, magicians, fire eaters and luminous ball throwers. Indoor laser shooting or casinos work well too (use pretend money). That way they can't drink at the same time.

The tax threshold for entertaining your employees is currently £75 per head.

Invite staff only, not their spouse or partner. For one thing, staff dos are boring for partners, and for another, spouses are an unknown quantity, so you can't be sure how they will behave.

Party boxes are a good idea. Put a big one in the middle of the table, surrounded by helium balloons, and fill it with crackers, balloons, party poppers and hats. They are fun for everyone to open.

Planning to party like there's no tomorrow? Well, there is one, so put a £20 note in an envelope in your pocket, with your home address on the front and simply hand it to the taxi driver at the end of the evening. Keeping the money in the envelope will ensure you aren't tempted to spend it at the bar.

Joined-up dancing
Lucy Pankhurst; Sarah Cramer; Jane Hodgkin, www.jivestories.com; Don McAlpine

If you are dancing socially and want to ask someone to dance, watch them for a while first to see what they're doing, as you have to be able to match your style to theirs. It might take a couple of dances to understand their style.

If you're a woman following the man's lead in a partner dance, you have to learn to concentrate on what your partner is doing. Watch and feel for the physical signs your partner is giving you, but at the same time, relax, and try not to anticipate what's coming next, or you could end up making a wrong assumption.

It can be daunting at first to lead a partner dance. Break down the dance in your mind, and have a few sequences ready. You can look great by recycling just a few steps in different combinations.

Remember that you can always mark time by going back to the basic step – you will always look good if you do it with energy and conviction.

Dancing a lot in high heels can damage your lower back, so wear flats whenever possible to compensate.

If you're going out dancing, you know you will get hot and sweaty, so when you're choosing your outfits, buy 2 or 3 tops that are identical. Nip to the loo to change in the middle of the evening – no one will know, because you're wearing exactly the same.

If you're not very fit, remember that you don't have to join a dance right at the beginning – you can wait 20 or 30 seconds, then join.

Always think about your stomach muscles. Hold them in, and you will look alert and poised without looking rigid. Make sure you can still breathe, though.

The popular myth that the man should always be taller – because otherwise the couple won't be able to dance well – is untrue. Don't worry if you're a short man or a tall woman; if you're both dancing well, you will both look good.

If a dance includes the woman turning under the man's arm, the woman should keep her head up so she looks confident, rather than ducking under his arm apologetically. If you are a tall woman, raise your arm higher to do this, as it also raises the man's arm.

To hold yourself straight while turning, feel your body as a column above the foot that you're turning on.

It actually takes very little energy to spin on one foot. If you put too much energy behind it, you can lose your balance. Use your partner's energy when they push you into a turn.

Turn your head quickly back to face your partner by turning your head faster than the rest of your body. This also stops you feeling dizzy.

Guests

How to Be a Good Host
Ivor Spencer, School for Butlers; Beryl Daniels

Sleep in your guest bedroom in advance – that way you'll know what's irritating and what's missing.

Give a lead on any plans well in advance so your guests can make sure they have the right clothes. If a country walk is on the cards, they will need suitable coats and footwear.

Warn smokers in advance if you don't like smoking in your house.

If your guests have small children and you don't, find out in advance what time they eat tea, have a bath and go to bed, so their routine doesn't clash with your social plans.

If your house has particular foibles (like strange plumbing) warn your guests; cold showers are no fun.

Leave a selection of blankets and enough pillows in the spare room so that guests can choose what suits them.

Put plenty of up-to-date magazines and books by their bed.

Supply tissues and a bottle of mineral water and glasses in their room. A hot-water bottle and an electric blanket would be useful too.

An alarm clock is a thoughtful gesture. But make sure it's one that doesn't tick.

Free some space in the wardrobe and empty drawers, or at the very least hang coat-hangers on the back of the door.

Make sure you show your guests their room when they arrive so that they can freshen up and unpack crushable clothes.

It's impolite to rush in and make your guest's bed. Live with an untidy room if that's the way they like it to be, for the duration of their stay.

Make it clear what time you clear away the breakfast.

Make allowances for vegetarians. Ask them when you first offer the invitation.

And if you are vegetarian, don't press your beliefs and spoil your guests' appetites.

Offer alternatives to post-dinner coffee, like

herbal teas and infusions.

Tell guests to help themselves; there is nothing worse than gasping for a cup of tea and not knowing if it's acceptable to help yourself.

Leave around a selection of newspapers, and don't feel pressurised into feeling you have to entertain your guests all the time.

Don't work your guests like slaves – they have come to you to be entertained …

… However, don't exhaust yourself by rushing around to keep them happy. A good guest will muck in and help.

Some people hate playing after-dinner games. Let them take a back seat if they are happier that way.

Make sure guests aren't left too long in an empty house. Leave details in their room of things to do and see.

Spoil your guests but let them relax and enjoy themselves – why else did you invite them?

How to Be a Good Guest

If you receive an invitation to a cocktail party, arrive about 10 minutes after the start time (not earlier than the start time) and leave at the time the invitation states.

When a dinner party invitation says 7.30 for 8, you must be there by 8. The hostess may have timed the dinner to be ready by then.

Flowers are a lovely present to take your hostess. A hand-tied bunch can be plopped straight into a vase and won't involve your hostess in having to arrange them.

Offered something you just can't eat? Cut it up small and move it around your plate, while you chat to other guests. It will probably be removed without comment.

If it is remarked on, say how much you enjoyed the meat/vegetables/sauce.

Leaving early is the height of rudeness unless you have a watertight excuse.

Overnight stays

Whether you are staying or have just been invited to dinner, a good bottle of champagne is always welcome, and it can be drunk then and there or kept for another day. A magnum is even better.

Find out how your hosts spend the day. That way you won't be caught out without clothes for church, a dressing gown for opening stockings before breakfast, etc.

Presents to take: make a contribution towards the catering, even if it's only after-dinner chocolates or a cake.

Offer to arrive with a meal. Perhaps a casserole for Christmas Eve which just needs reheating in the oven. Don't arrive with elaborate ingredients that need assembling.

Spoil your host and hostess by giving them a silk scarf or expensive tie. People can never have too many of these.

Over Christmas your hosts will have gone to lots of expense, so an armful of presents would be thoughtful: home-made chutneys, bath oils or soaps, a plant or a special cutting (but remember that they won't have time to do anything with it until after Christmas).

Think about their hobbies. Everyone – even a non-gardener – has room for a plant or small tree in their garden. It's a thoughtful present but see above.

You can never have too many photos either. Frame a picture taken of the family during the year.

Don't forget their children. If you are clueless about what to give them, book tokens suit any age.

Don't turn up with an uninvited guest – human or otherwise.

If you have any special dietary requirements, make sure your hostess knows well in advance.

Take your own towel and dressing gown.

A good guest mucks in – and doesn't sit back, waiting to be entertained. Rather than say, 'What can I do to help?' check whether the log basket is empty/fire needs laying/table needs setting and say, 'Why don't I do that?'

'You can't poke someone's fire unless you've known them for 7 years. You can't be rude to their dogs unless you've known them for 14 years.'

Do ask before hogging the television-channel remote control.

Check your host's policy on smoking before lighting up, and resist if it's obvious they would rather you didn't. Just offer to walk the dog a lot!

Offers to walk the dog are a host's dream come true, as is time spent enter-taining their children.

Check it's all right to have a bath – so that you don't leave the household with cold water.

Don't help yourself to the kettle, drinks or the fridge without asking first.

Praise your host and hostess, but try not to gush.

Send your hosts pictures of your stay.

Own up to breakages and offer to com-pensate. Back down with grace if the offer is refused.

Check you haven't left anything behind, otherwise your hostess will have to arrange for items to be posted back to you. Take an extra empty suitcase for packing any presents you receive so that they don't get lost.

Thank-you letters are a must.

'After three days, guests and fish stink.'
John Lyle

A good guest doesn't complain.

Photography and Video
Alex Fraser

Don't film or photograph somebody directly in front of a window – it may look fine through the viewfinder, but you'll probably end up with a silhouette that looks more like an identity parade for axe murderers.

People never think enough about sound. If you're going to actually edit your home video rushes, sound is as important as pictures. If a phone is ringing or birds are singing, get what's called a 'wild track' – that is, a minute or so of recorded sound – that you can then dub over one or two successive shots, instead of the phone suddenly cutting in, then out, or a bird bursting into song from nowhere, then seemingly dropping dead.

Want to achieve that professional look when a shot is 'tracking' – that is, the camera seems to be moving to keep up with the action? Just use a supermarket trolley; rest the camera on the child seat for a steady effect. Try not to get one with a wobbly wheel.

Invest in a tripod. They are ideal for taking family snaps that even the photographer wants to appear in, and hand-held video camera shots never ever look really steady.

If you're low on batteries, avoid those flip-out monitors that many cameras have now. Use the viewfinder instead. The flip-out monitors eat up power.

Different temperatures can affect your camera. If you come in from the cold to the heat, always allow your camera a few minutes to 'acclimatise'.

Home videos often look amateur because we just shoot too much of everything we see. Be selective; professional cameramen take time to choose the right shot, the best backdrop and the right framing.

If you're filming children, come down to their eye level. You'll get a more attractive shot and probably a better 'performance'.

Vary your height of shooting in general. Stand on a chair, get down on your knees or change the actual angle of the camera. It will all make for a much more interesting final video or photograph.

The laziest shot is the 'mid shot' – that is, from the head to the tummy button, and usually with lots of empty space around the person. Experiment with very tight close-ups on faces for dramatic or personal moments – or allow your subject to move around rather than being fixed to the spot, for a bit of fun.

Family, Children and Pets

Family Therapy
Jill Curtis, Family Therapist, Family2000; Ros Graham

Enjoyable family rituals are crucial to family health and well-being. What makes family rituals a positive experience is the meaning created in the family, and the bonding that occurs between family members.

Make family rituals intentional rather than something that happens by default. Make a plan, make sure everyone knows what's going to happen and stick to it, with everyone playing a part.

Coordinate the making of the ritual so that all family members are participants. Shopping for the food, making the Christmas dinner, setting the table and the clean-up afterwards should all be shared responsibilities. A special shopping trip to gather the food and assigning responsibilities can help make your Christmas a family affair. Feeling responsible for the creation of the ritual strengthens each individual member's bond to the family group.

Consider the role of extended family, friends and community in your family

ritual. Connection to community is one of the key elements of a successful family ritual. The Christmas holidays are an excellent opportunity to invite special friends and relatives to contribute to your family's event. Other activities, such as helping at a soup kitchen, or donating food to others in need, can also reinforce your family's connection to a greater whole.

Repetition and flexibility: remember that rituals are defined by repetition. A family event needs to be repeated three times for it to become a ritual with a spirit of its own in your family. When a ritual is truly established, all members take ownership for its continuation. This ensures that even when a family ritual is missed one year, another family member insists on it the next. Not only do these rituals have to be repeated, but they must also reflect the needs of your growing family.

Responsibilities may shift over the years. It is possible that your teenagers will do the cooking in years ahead. The key to maintaining the active and positive participation of all members is to strike a healthy balance which allows all individuals to experience meaning and connection. Willingness to be flexible assures that the ritual remains intact and meaningful to all of its members through the years.

Troubleshoot problem areas in your family's rituals. If your family event is dull, filled with negative tension or does not impart the positive experience you desire, do not despair. Simply ask yourselves what is missing or what changes are needed to create meaning and connection. If your children are bored by the length of time the turkey takes to cook, what about initiating a change, like a nature walk or family game as a part of the Christmas festivities? If conflict arises between family members, can an agreement be made to save the discussion for after the family ritual?

The making of your family rituals are a work in progress. Consciously protect your family celebrations from divisive tensions. Stresses will naturally occur. Keep in mind that your overall goal is to experience enough warmth and enjoyment that the end result is that family members want to spend time together. Satisfying family rituals are not just a good idea. They help ensure that your family relationships endure throughout the life cycle.

Make each Christmas memorable in some way for each person in the family. A biscuit or sweet tin, emptied during the festive period, can be used as a 'time capsule' for the family, with everyone writing a message and putting in an object of significance. Take a photo of everyone to include, and put it away until next year.

Cut off a piece about 10mm (half an inch) thick from the stump of your Christmas tree. Write the date on it and screw a picture hook into the back. As the collection grows, attach each piece to a strong ribbon, and you'll have a garland that goes on growing each year.

Buy a special decoration each year that reflects that year of your lives. For example, for the birth of a child, look out for a cherub decoration; for a house move, buy a little wooden building. This way, every decoration has a special meaning.

Create family calendars using photographs taken during the previous year. This makes a great gift that keeps the previous year's memories fresh in everyone's minds.

Go out as a family to a film or play that everyone can enjoy, then eat out together and have a good chat – about the show if that's the easiest topic. Combine it with a trip to look at the Christmas lights and the shop windows for a simple, stress-free family get-together.

Create a memory bag – a little bag with a drawstring that can hang on the tree. Each year the family members record the outstanding memory of the year and it goes into the bag to be kept. Then read them all out after Christmas dinner.

Ask everyone coming for the Christmas meal to bring a poem or story to read out loud. Take it in turns to read the poems as a gift to each other.

On Christmas Eve, read or even act out the Christmas story, involving everyone – even pets – to the best of their ability. Make sure to video the result on a special tape and show them all each year on Christmas Day.

On New Year's Eve make a list of things you would like to accomplish in the New Year. These should be positive – praying together, keeping bedrooms clean, etc. – and activities you would like to do – projects, fairs, the zoo, etc. Several times throughout the year review your list to see how you're doing.

Make a 'Christmas memories' scrapbook every year, starting this year. Take plenty of pictures, and get disposable cameras for children to use themselves. Stick the pictures in together and write captions to help keep the memories fresh.

Choose something special, that everyone enjoys, for breakfast on Christmas Day. The scent of tangerines and coffee are very evocative.

If you take your kids to see Father Christmas, make sure you take a picture, then display the pictures every year as part of your decorations. It's fun to see how the children have grown.

Make getting the tree a tradition rather than a chore. Get everyone involved in choosing it and give yourself plenty of time.

Make decorating it an activity that everyone can enjoy, not an exercise in aesthetic perfection.

Instead of saying a traditional grace, ask each person at the dinner table say at least one thing that they are grateful for that day. This makes everyone pause and it really keeps the mood up when you have to think of what went right during your day rather than focusing on what went wrong. It is especially challenging for the adults!

Collect a little something for the tree during any holiday throughout the year – shells from the beach, paper flags or souvenirs from your summer holiday – all help to remind everyone of the good times through the previous months.

Drink can cause people to become aggressive or maudlin. Try not to start too early.

If you spread present opening through the day, this will stop excitement levels boiling over.

Alternatively, set aside a specific time for children to open presents, and give them your attention. They will then be happy to go and play while you get on with other chores.

Don't be ruled by traditions. Make your own Christmas traditions, which contribute to what therapists call anchoring – this helps people feel they 'belong'.

Just because you did Christmas a certain way last year doesn't mean you have to do the same this year. Vary your routine – perhaps have dinner instead of lunch, go to the midnight service so you can have a lie-in, or even plan to go away.

Forget the rules: when else can you eat chocolate in bed?

Keep your expectations low – if you don't expect your children (or your mother-in-law) to behave, then you won't be frustrated when they don't.

If you are the hosts, don't feel obliged to entertain everyone all the time. You will end up tired and angry. Set the scene and let others make an effort and lend a hand. Be happy giving people tasks to do.

And give others space too. If children are happy playing quietly with their new toys, leave them to it. People will get angry if they feel they are being dragooned into activities.

Allow yourself a get-out clause. Many people stuck together under one roof can cause cabin fever. Put on your wellies and get fresh air, walk the dog, visit a neighbour … Give yourself space.

Make sure there are plenty of fairy lights. According to Feng Shui, they create positive energy.

Psychologists say that yelling is a good release of pent-up energy. Involve the family in games like Pictionary or charades where they can shout.

Ban sulking.

To avoid problems with an extended family, start communicating well in advance with all the adults involved. Find out what the stepchildren, half-siblings and other kids want, so that you don't double up.

Make sure all the children have about the same number of presents. It can cause a lot of trouble if some are still opening gifts after others have finished.

Ask the children how they feel about the arrangements, and make sure they know where they are going to be and when. There may be some detail that is tiny to you but which is incredibly important to them and which can easily be altered to keep everyone happy.

Keep plenty of spare films so you can photograph all permutations of your extended family. It can be very hurtful, looking back on the pictures, to find you've been missed out.

Don't expect too much. If you can please some of the people some of the time, you've succeeded.

Include some treats for yourself – even tiny ones will do – or you'll spend the whole of Christmas feeling like a martyr.

Keeping Children Happy
Revd William Stileman

Chocolate and sweets, eaten early in the morning from stockings, can cause children to go ballistic. Try to keep their intake to the minimum.

If toys need assembly, ensure they are assembled before you wrap them. That way, you won't have children jumping from one leg to the other while you try to wrestle with the instructions.

Make sure Santa leaves his mark. Sprinkle some talc or flour in the hearth so that his big boots will leave a footprint when he comes.

Some children can be terrified by the idea of Father Christmas coming into their bedroom. Leave their stocking by the fireside instead – it seems unfair to expect him to traipse around the house anyway. He's a busy man.

Ease off the roller-coaster of excitement. Let children have a quiet time with their toys, rather than expecting them to join in all the time.

Children and church can be a bad mix. Try to choose one where children are positively welcomed, and go armed with colouring pencils and paper to keep younger ones happy during the slower parts.

Alternatively, get them to add up the sum of all the hymn numbers.

Or play the alphabet game during the sermon. Older children have to go through the alphabet in the right order and tick off each letter every time the vicar says a word beginning with that letter. Count 'ex' as 'x' (Xerxes doesn't often get mentions in Christmas sermons). It will certainly make them listen to the words!

Crib services on Christmas Eve are often very interactive, and involvement is much more encouraged than during a Mass or communion.

Let children dress up as shepherds/angels, and make it a fun part of the Christmas celebrations.

Dressing-up clothes

Get your children involved in helping to make dressing-up clothes. It will double the fun.

Don't throw out old sheets, curtains, worn-out clothes or offcuts until you have explored all the possibilities for recycling them.

Even if the material you have doesn't look very promising, bear in mind that dye can transform a fabric beyond recognition.

Look in charity shops and at jumble sales for suitable garments and fabrics.

Keep a selection of interesting buttons, particularly large or metallic ones.

Make angel wings from wire coat-hangers, pulled to shape and wrapped with tinsel. Sew on to thick elastic and attach to a vest.

Pet Care During Christmas
Nick Horniman MRCVS, Pets Barn Veterinary Centres and Animal Hospitals, Gloucestershire

Don't leave wrapped-up chocolate or other edible gifts under the Christmas tree, as pets will open and eat them. Chocolate for humans contains a substance that is toxic to dogs.

Stomach upsets in pets are common during the Christmas period. Baking foil can cut open a dog's intestines if eaten and rich food gives them diarrhoea. Bones get stuck in the throat and can pierce the gut, so be aware of what your pet might be able to reach.

Many dogs get fat from overfeeding and under-exercise over Christmas. Stick to their normal diet and don't be tempted to give out festive treats. Walk the dog rather than watch the same James Bond movie you saw last year.

'A dog is for life ... etc.' holds very true; pets don't make good presents. Many breeders will not sell just before Christmas.

Over-excitement could cause your dog to accidentally bite children. Allow cooling-down time and the opportunity for your pet to escape the children if it wants to.

Going away and using kennels for your pet? Make arrangements early, use one recommended by a friend, visit it before you use it. Make sure you are comfortable with the facilities.

If you are going away, house sitters are a good idea. They will look after your pet and your home.

Cats like to climb trees, so use non-breakable tree decorations.

Cats have been known to chew and swallow curly ribbons from presents. Be careful.

If you are leaving cats during the day, leave a litter tray, food and water. Make the house safe, and ask a neighbour to call in to check them.

The same applies to dogs, but you should not leave a dog at home alone all day. Make sure the dog doesn't bark when left alone or you won't be popular with the neighbours.

Party poppers can get eaten. They can also frighten and injure pets, especially their eyes. Use proper care.

Crackers too could scare them and the toys inside could get eaten, causing poisoning and blockages.

Fireworks terrify pets. Make sure your pet is shut in the house, as far away from the noise as possible.

Christmas decoration foliage and berries could be poisonous (for children too). Take care not to let it fall down or be within reach of pets.

When candles are lit, take care not to allow cats to jump up and knock the candle over. Christmas decorations can be flammable.

Don't let pets chew the wires to Christmas tree lights. Use the cardboard inner tube from rolls of wrapping paper to protect it.

Vacuum up fallen needles from the tree regularly as they could get stuck in your pets' feet.

Wildlife at Christmas
Colin Studholme, The Gloucestershire Wildlife Trust

Give a thought to the birds and wild animals. During the Christmas holidays, make ornaments from berries, bread, peanut butter, honey, and birdseed. Then take them out into the forest and hide them around in the trees and bushes for all the birds and animals.

Birds need feeding during the winter. Hang bird-quality peanuts (not the salted kind) in a branch or from a bird table (blue tits love them). Remember to leave water too but make sure it is kept ice-free.

The greater the variety of food you leave out, the greater the variety of birds you will attract. Greenfinches love sunflower seeds, whereas blackbirds, thrushes, redwings and fieldfares love to peck at apples, pears and other fruits scattered on the ground.

Scatter food in the corners of the patio for secretive feeders like wrens and dunnocks.

Birds love bacon rind, but avoid dry bread, as this can become stuck in their throats.

Keep the bird table clean and away from bushes where cats can lurk.

Once you start feeding birds, don't stop. They will come to rely on you.

Use plastic berries for decorations in the house. Leave the real ones on the trees for the birds.

Keep an eye out for the welfare of fish in garden ponds too. Break ice as it forms on the top of the water.

Going Away

Security in the Home
Police

When out for the day

Don't leave presents where they can be seen through a window.

Put lights on timers and ask a neighbour to come in and close the curtains for you.

Use plug-in time-switches on lamps because they go on and off automatically. However, take care to vary the setting on each time-switch so that they don't all come on and go off at once.

When you are in one evening, go outside and see how your house looks from the outside. That is how it should look at night when you are away.

Windows and patio doors are particularly vulnerable and should be secured with key-operated locks or screws. All animal or cat flaps, no matter how small, should be sealed.

You can stop intruders from shinning up pipes and on to low roofs by applying anti-climb grease and by removing objects outside (such as ladders) that could make climbing easier.

Outside lights with passive infra-red detectors are easy to fit these days and are useful deterrents to would-be burglars because they are triggered by body movement.

When away over Christmas

The best approach is to plan well ahead and make a list of those things that must be done to secure your home. Inform everyone who needs to know that you will be away, but avoid letting strangers know; you may be helping the burglar choose his next target. The following checklist should help you avoid his attentions.

Have you:
- *Arranged for pets to be properly cared for?* Your local branch of the RSPCA, pet shop or vet will be able to advise you on kennels, catteries, etc.
- *Locked all doors and windows?*
- *Locked the shed and/or garage* and put all tools away?
- *Told your neighbours you will be away?*

Give them your holiday address in case of emergency.

- **Asked your neighbours to remove any post** or newspapers left showing in the letterbox, and put some rubbish in your dustbin?
- **Turned off the gas and water supply?** Turn off the electricity unless you need it for a freezer, time switches, etc.
- **Cancelled milk and newspapers**, bread and other regular deliveries?
- **Deposited at the bank** small items of value, such as jewellery and quantities of cash?
- **Considered time-switches** to operate lights during the hours of darkness to give the impression the house is occupied?

Put yourself in the burglar's position. How would you get in if you were locked out? The chances are that a burglar will use the same route!

If you are away over Christmas, you may not think it's worth bothering to decorate, but a house that looks empty and tinsel-free is an open invitation to an intruder. It might be worth hanging a wreath on the door or a paper chain in the window.

Take particular care when going out to parties, and especially midnight carol services. Burglars have no scruples and know there are probably presents waiting under the tree. Leave all the lights on and the radio playing to act as a deterrent.

To secure your home against the opportunist burglar who steals cash and any valuable items that are on view:

- *Check* the locks of ground-floor doors and windows.
- *Check* that any upstairs windows that overlook flat roofs or balconies have locks.
- *Check* that garage doors are locked.
- *Check* the security of shed doors and windows.

If you live in a flat or maisonette you should also check the main communal-entrance security and the security of skylights.

Detached houses are more at risk than semi-detached or terraced properties. This is because they are often secluded, and neighbours may not be able to see or hear burglars at work.

Houses or flats that are near the ends of streets or that back on to alleyways, parks, fields, or waste ground are also particularly at risk, because of the ease of access.

Walls, fences and shrubs around the garden may give you greater privacy, but they also enable the burglar to work unnoticed.

Patio doors give you a good view out, but they can provide an easy way into your home.

Nothing worth stealing? Remember that, in most cases, before burglars enter a home, they don't know what they'll find to steal. Burglars will assume that you do have something they want, and once they're inside they'll find something to make the risk of being caught worthwhile.

They may steal cash or jewellery, TVs or videos, computers, cameras or antiques. These days even the contents of an average home freezer are often worth a second look to a thief, especially if it is unlocked. The top 10 items on the burglar's shopping list are:

Money
Jewellery
Chequebooks and credit cards
Antiques
Cameras
Silverware
Video recorders
Televisions
Hi-fi equipment
Computers

SAFEGUARDING COMPUTERS AND GAMES CONSOLES

When you take delivery of a new computer or games console don't put stacks of empty hardware boxes outside on bin day – it advertises to thieves that there are new machines inside.

Try to avoid leaving computers near windows: for a start it's not good for them to get too much sun, and it also makes it easy for thieves to see what you've got.

Take software out of boxes and keep disks in a different place to manuals. It makes them far less attractive to thieves who can sell boxed sets with instruction manuals at car boot fairs.

Dos and don'ts

Do: lock all your doors and windows when you go out. Pay particular attention to the rear of your premises – a popular entry point for burglars.

Don't: leave door keys in hiding places, such as under the doormat or in a flowerpot. Thieves know all the hiding places.

Do: fit good-quality rim and/or mortice locks to all external doors, and use a 'deadlock' on the front door. Use mortice security bolts or key-operated door-security press bolts on the top and bottom of both solid wood and glazed back doors.

Don't: leave a window open a few inches for the cat to get in or out. Burglars find this very useful too.

Do: keep your shed and/or garage locked. Your tools are useful to the thief who wants to gain entry. If your garage has a communicating door with the interior of the house, secure it as you would another exterior door.

Don't: leave ladders lying around. If you must keep them outside, padlock them to something secure so that you are the only person who can use them.

Do: close the curtains and leave a light on in a room (not the hall) when you are out for the evening. *Remember* also to close curtains when you are in, so that the burglar cannot see where you are.

Do: leave a radio on – but with a talk programme, rather than music.

Don't: leave curtains and blinds drawn during the daytime; they attract the thief.

Do: illuminate dark areas around your home. Remember: burglars hate light.

Don't: leave 'back soon' notes on display. Burglars love a written guarantee that the house is unoccupied.

Do: make sure that your house and contents are insured.

Don't: forget to mark your valuables with your postcode/house number, and make sure that you display a sticker showing that you have done so. Marked property is less attractive to the thief and is harder to dispose of. Photograph all items of high value, and record serial numbers of televisions, video recorders, cameras, etc. Have a ruler in shot so that the size of the object can be gauged.

Do: fit locks to all windows on the ground floor, as well as those on the first floor that can be easily reached from flat roofs or drainpipes. If you haven't got window locks, you can buy them (they're not expensive) from locksmiths, hardware stores, DIY stores and builders' merchants. Choose locks that secure the opening sections to the main frames. They are effective because even if the glass is broken, the window can't easily be opened, and a burglar won't normally bother to take out all the glass. It takes too long, makes too much noise and increases the risk of being caught.

Patio doors should be fitted with extra security locks, top and bottom, and anti-lift devices, which prevent doors from being lifted off the rails.

Louvre windows are particularly vulnerable because the glass slats can be easily removed. If you have this type of window, gluing the slats to the frames with strong adhesive (epoxy resin – not superglue) will make it far more difficult for the burglar. There are special locks available too.

All doors, but especially outward opening doors, should have hinge bolts fitted. For the best protection on front main doors, you should fit a security deadlock which preferably conforms to BS 3621. Look for the British Standard Kite Mark if you're not sure. Most insurers now require locks to BS 3621.

When choosing a locksmith, you should ensure that the locks and bolts they supply and the quality of their installation reach British Standards specifications BS 3621. This will mean that they meet the requirements of your insurance company.

Travelling Over Christmas
AA

Car maintenance

It's worth having a service done before winter arrives, to avoid possible problems.

Make sure you change the antifreeze in the radiator at 2-year intervals.

If the battery is more than 4 years old, have it checked before the winter chills set in, especially if the engine begins to labour when you start it up.

Switch off all electrical accessories before starting the car. Use the starter in bursts of not more than 5 seconds, with 30-second gaps if the car does not start promptly.

Boost the screenwash with up to 50 per cent methylated spirits to prevent freezing.

If you leave the engine running to warm it up, switch the wipers off – ice can damage the rubber and the wiper motor can overheat.

If the locks freeze, carefully heat the lock and the key (with a cigarette lighter or your hands), but do not blow into the lock, as condensation makes the problem worse.

Tyre grip is critical in the winter months, so check regularly for wear, cuts and damage. Servicing should include a tyre check, but it's up to you to maintain the correct pressure and ensure that tyres have at least 3–4mm of tread. If it's down to 2mm, change the tyre; 1.6mm is the legal limit.

Don't reduce your tyre pressure; it does not enhance grip and will also reduce stability.

Diesel car? Should you expect severe conditions, make sure you use a proper winter-grade fuel.

Essential items for the car in winter: torch, jack and wheel wrench, warning triangle, snow shovel, first-aid kit, blanket, water dispersant fluid, vacuum flask and, most importantly, warm coat and boots!

Pamper your car over the Christmas holidays; leaving the car idle for a few days could result in a flat battery. Try to get out at some stage and take the car for a good run.

Put a can of water repellent on your Christmas list. If the engine gives up the ghost, wipe down the battery leads, distributor cap and ignition coil (in older cars), before spraying the entire area.

Presents for your car:
- **Battery jump leads** – could come in handy if your battery is flat.
- **Water repellent** – ideal for getting damp engines ticking over.
- **Antifreeze** – in readiness for the cold snap.
- **Screenwash** – keeps your windscreen muck-free.
- **Engine oil** – an absolute must for any motorist.
- **Ice scraper** – beats using a credit card!
- **Wellington boots** – handy in floods, or even snow.
- **Travel blanket** – provides warmth if your car breaks down.

Travelling abroad
Caroline Whaley

There are few advantages to travelling over Christmas, and in the run-up to the day, planes and trains can be packed (always book a seat on the latter).

But if you don't mind arriving at your destination on Christmas Day itself, you'll find the flights much emptier, even if no cheaper.

Fly from west to east and you could end up with 2 (or even 3) Christmas dinners!

Going from east to west, on the other hand, may mean you miss out on Christmas Day altogether.

Skiing
Vanessa Haines, Ski Club of Great Britain (www.skiclub.co.uk); Bernard Cheek

Beginners should take at least one dry-slope lesson before heading to the mountains.

Try to do some pre-ski exercises or, if this fails, have a quick stretch before you head down the slopes. Try to remember to stretch again before going to bed – it will ease aching muscles.

Remember to take spare films for your camera – film can be expensive and difficult to get hold of in small resorts.

Save weight in your main bag and protect

your skis when travelling by packing clothes around your skis in a ski bag.

Buy a double ski bag to save money; it will carry 2 pairs of skis (and give you extra room in which to stuff socks and undies).

Tie a bright strip of ribbon or tape around your boot bag to recognise it when travelling. Hundreds of skiers and snow-boarders have the same boot bags.

Wear lots of thin layers as opposed to one thick layer under your ski jacket.

Mittens can keep your hands warmer than gloves.

Hand and boot warmers make life more pleasant on cold snowy days.

Woollen socks are far more comfortable than synthetic.

Sports bras are every girl's essential item for negotiating a mogul field.

Never ski without sunglasses or goggles – they prevent snow-blindness.

Goggles rather than sunglasses will enable you to see better in white-out weather.

Always wear high-factor sun cream; even when it's cloudy, light reflects off the snow and can still burn your face.

Take a few boiled sweets up the moun-

tain with you – they provide an excellent boost when you're getting tired.

Take a roll from breakfast and make a sandwich for lunch – this will save you money at lunchtime.

Remember, however, that many Europeans will not be happy if you start eating your own picnic at their mountain restaurants.

European restaurants will sometimes charge a small sum for toilet entry – check that you have small change before heading down to the loos.

If wearing an all-in-one, tie the arms together when going to the loo so they don't drag on the floor.

Ease off on alcohol on some nights – the high altitude dehydrates the body anyway – and drink plenty of water before hitting the sack.

Don't sit down on a button lift – let the poma gradually pull you up the hill.

Always carry skis on your shoulder with the front end of the skis pointing forwards.

Undo back and or side clips on your boots to ease walking.

If you fall and your skis come off, always lay your skis across the slope and put the lower one on first.

Before heading off the piste, make sure you are wearing an avalanche transceiver and that it is switched to the 'transmit' mode.

Don't go off the piste without a guide – it just isn't worth it.

If you're inexperienced at off-piste skiing, rent 'fat boys' (broad skis) to make life easier.

At the end of your skiing holiday, make sure your skis are dry before packing them away. Damp skis will rust along the edges.

A Bit of Pampering

Looking Good Over Christmas
Woman and Home Magazine

Prepare yourself for the party season by booking yourself in for an energy-boosting massage. Choose one that doesn't leave you covered in oil either, so that you can slip into your party dress afterwards.

No time for a massage? Add a few drops of energy-boosting aromatherapy oil (containing rosemary, bergamot or juniper) to your bath. Don't run the water too hot or you will actually drain your energy.

Give your hair and your face a mask treatment.

You can buy wash-out colour sachets from the chemist to give yourself a temporary new look.

Before a big party, treat yourself to a wash and blow-dry at the hairdresser. They will also be able to put up long hair so that it lasts for the evening. If you have long thin hair, make sure the appointment is late in the afternoon.

Apply your perfume before you blow-dry your hair. This will diffuse the scent and help it to calm down.

Cheat with fake tan, but practise a few days ahead to ensure the colour is right for you. Exfoliate your skin before applying fake tan and it will last longer.

If you plan to dance the night away, prepare your feet with a deep-moisturising foot cream, keep toe nails short and filed (it's easier to do this straight after a bath when they are soft), then apply nail polish.

If you plan to drink alcohol, drink plenty of water too, to stop yourself dehydrating.

Use a quick-dry top-coat nail polish to stop smudging.

To prevent clogged eyelashes, replace your mascara every 6 weeks.

For long-lasting glossy lips, apply a layer of lipstick, then blot with tissue. Apply another coat and blot again, then apply gloss just to the middle of your lower lip.

Try not to press lips together after applying lipstick – it will make your lipstick 'bleed'.

Pumping your mascara wand in and out of the tube pushes in air and eventually dries out the mascara.

To test a foundation, apply it to your jawline, not your hand (the skin is a different colour there).

Keep a powder compact in your handbag to disguise a shiny nose.

Cold wintry weather and centrally heated houses can have a very drying effect on the skin. Keep your skin supple and soft over Christmas by applying a good moisturiser (it doesn't have to be expensive) morning and night. Protect lips with Vaseline when out walking. Stand a ramekin of water with a few drops of lavender oil on a radiator to fragrance and humidify the atmosphere in one go.

When looking for a really glamorous evening dress, it's a good idea to be fitted for a fabulous bra which will give you the shape you love, then buy the dress to show off your shape! (Needless to say, always try on the dress wearing your super bra!)

Make-up
Nyki Collins; Shannon Keogh; Françoise de Pigny

If you're going to be in a hot room and you have a tendency to become 'shiny', make it look deliberate! Wear lip gloss and sheen on your eyelids.

To keep your make-up fresh, however hot the conditions, use a quick spray of water every so often.

Loose powder often looks too heavy because it sticks to moisturisers and cleansers. Blot your face with a tissue before you put any powder on.

The oil from your skin can affect the powder in your compact. Store the powder puff or sponge face upwards, towards the mirror.

Alternatively, apply loose powder with throw-away cotton-wool pads. The puff provided with the powder will quickly build up dirt and won't do your skin any favours.

If you've got a reddish complexion, use a foundation with a greenish tinge. Applied under normal make-up, this will help to neutralise the red.

If you've got a really, really bad spot, you'll never be able to cover it up for a party. Instead, turn it into a trendy beauty spot with a dark eyeliner pencil.

Get better coverage from your foundation by tapping it into place instead of blending it.

To make blusher look more natural, tilt your head downwards until you naturally blush and use the blush areas as guidelines.

Minimalist make-up bag: rather than

spending a fortune on cosmetics, invest in
just a plain glossy lip colour and use on
eyes and lips, then touch up lashes with
mascara.

Luscious lips

**To get the deepest, longest-lasting effect
from lipstick**, powder your lips before applying it.

Alternatively, apply lipstick, dust with
powder, then apply another layer. Both techniques will make lipstick last longer.

For long-lasting matt lip colour, line the
entire lips with lip liner. Add a coat of lip
balm to moisturise the lips.

To get a perfect lip line with lip liner,
place the pencil in a glass of warm/hot water
(with its cap on) for about 5 minutes, then
apply as usual.

When applying lipstick, do it with a brush
following the contours of your lips, then
define with a lip pencil in the same shade
and blot with a tissue.

A thin layer of Vaseline will moisturise
very dry lips under lipstick.

Test if you've overdone the lipstick by
putting your finger gently into your mouth
and pulling it out again. If there are any traces
on your finger, you've applied too much.

You can change the colour of a lipstick by

adding face toner with an eyeshadow brush.

To mend a broken lipstick, carefully melt the broken edges with a lighted match and press them together. Smooth down the join with a toothpick and then leave the lipstick in the fridge for a couple of hours.

The eyes have it

When applying moisturiser, avoid the eye area. Not only is the skin more delicate but you will coat the lashes with oil and your mascara will smudge.

Eyeliners need to be really sharp. Try chilling eye pencils in the fridge before sharpening them to get a really good point.

Avoid smudgy eyeliner by dipping a wet brush in dark eye shadow and using this to line the eyes instead. It will stay on all day (and all night).

When applying mascara, look down directly into a mirror. It makes it impossible to get mascara into the eyes.

After applying mascara, spray a little hairspray on to the brush and apply a layer to the lashes (avoid this if you have very sensitive eyes).

If your mascara is too runny, leave the lid off overnight to dry it out a bit.

When you run out of mascara, stand the tube in a cup of hot water for 1 minute. This will loosen the last bit of mascara and allow you to use it for at least 2 more coats.

To lighten the colour of cream eye shadows, cream blusher and lipstick, mix with some concealer.

Before you do anything radical when colouring eyebrows, apply some coloured mascara to see the effect. Eyebrow pencil works well too.

Thick eyebrows? Clear mascara will keep brows neatly in place.

Run out of eye make-up remover? Use petroleum jelly or Vaseline instead. This even works for waterproof mascara.

Hands and Nails
Midge A. Killen, Amazing Nails, USA; Lynn Shaw at Nailtiques; Mandy Rouse, Beautique, Stratford-upon-Avon

Dipping your nails in warm olive oil will moisturise them, soften the cuticles and help stop them splitting.

If your hands are stained or discoloured, rub the skin with half a lemon. Rinse off and dry your hands carefully, then massage in some hand cream, because lemon has a drying effect on the skin.

If you get ink stains on your hands, rub the stains with a nailbrush that you have dipped in vinegar and salt. You could also try rubbing the ink stains with the inside of a banana skin.

Clean grubby nails – especially if you're a smoker – with minted toothpaste.

Push back cuticles with lollipop sticks.

For heavy-duty hand cream, mix together virgin olive oil and petroleum jelly. Rub the mixture into your hands and then put them into freezer bags. Sit and have a cuppa or read the paper while your hands absorb the benefits of this perfect conditioner.

Don't wipe away excess hand cream – rub it into the cuticles and let it soak in.

For a home-made exfoliator, mix 1 teaspoon olive oil with salt to make a paste and massage it over the hands. To remove, rinse the hands under warm to hot water. This leaves hands feeling like silk. This natural exfoliant is ideal for gardeners, as the salt removes the dirt and the oil rehydrates the skin.

Avoid nail fungus by cleaning your manicuring tools in antibacterial soap.

Always style nails when wearing hand cream, as this protects the nails. Remember that nails are most vulnerable when filing.

When filing nails, keep going in one direction. Sawing backwards and forwards weakens the edges.

Always wear nail polish when shaping nails for home manicure, as it makes it easier to see the shape you are creating. It also avoids splitting or breaking them.

Stop the top of the nail varnish from sticking – just rub some petroleum jelly on to the top of the bottle.

Keep nail varnish in the fridge – it lasts for much longer.

Avoid bubbles in your nail varnish by gently rolling the bottle to even out the colour, rather than shaking it as we all do.

Stop nails discolouring by using a colour-less base coat first.

To make short nails look longer, use darker shades of nail varnish, and don't paint the edges of your nails.

Metallic nail colours make small nails look bigger.

Try a classic French polish. The white-tipped manicure works just as well on toes, creating a clean, well-maintained look.

Colour the tip of the nail first with nail polish. It will make it last longer.

Clear nail varnish applied on top of colour will help it last longer too.

The new fast-drying nail varnishes can make your nails go yellow if used constantly. Once in a while give your nails a break from polish altogether; just rub in some almond oil and give them a really good buffing.

In a hurry? Run newly polished nails under cold water or dip in iced water to help them dry more quickly.

Dipping them in baby oil works well too.

Remove any stains left by nail varnish by dipping your nails into fresh lemon juice.

Perfume
Floris; Caroline Samuels

Make sure your perfume is working for you. For maximum effectiveness, always apply it to your pulse points, where the blood circulates closest to the surface. Your pulse points are: behind the ears, the nape of the neck, inside the wrists, the temples, the crook of the elbow, behind the knees and on the ankles. Perfume rises, so putting it on your lower body works well.

When in doubt, apply perfume to where you expect to be kissed!

The higher the concentration of perfume, the longer the scent lasts – and the more expensive it is, because it contains a greater percentage of essential fragrance oils. Extract or perfume has the highest concentration, followed by parfum de toilette and eau de parfum, then eau de toilette, eau de cologne and, lowest of all, splash cologne.

However, because the fragrance content of perfume or eau de parfum is that much higher, you do not need so much of it to obtain the same effect. It will also be longer lasting on the skin.

What makes perfume last? This is determined by the blend of base-note essential oils and fixatives used. Lighter fragrances, by their very nature, do not contain the base-note essential oils that create more lasting power on the skin.

To create a 'voile' or veil of perfume, spray one or more fragrances into the air and walk through the perfume cloud. It creates a subtle layer of fragrance all over your body, hair and clothes.

Spray a little of your favourite perfume on to your hairbrush and then brush your hair.

Want to treat a girlfriend to fragrance for Christmas? Take a sneaky look at her favourites in her bathroom, then give her the talc, body lotion, etc. that go with it.

Shopping for Clothes
Catherine Fenwick, Dickins & Jones, London; Sally Fabian

Look the part: if you are going out to shop for an evening dress, wear the right underwear and take favourite necklaces and/or earrings with you to get the full effect.

The right underwear means a flesh-coloured thong and a flesh-coloured bra.

Ask to take the garment to the door.

Shop lights can distort colour and you should see the item in daylight. This is especially important if you are buying something black.

Always buy shoes in the morning. By afternoon, your feet will have swollen.

New party shoes? Wear them in around the house well before the event.

And when buying shoes, wear tights.

It's a disaster to impulse buy and is rarely a success.

Try to remember what you have in your wardrobe at home and don't duplicate it when you're out shopping. You can also buy to complement what you already have.

If the budget is tight, buy one good evening dress (a little black number perhaps) and change it with scarves, earrings, necklaces.

Take off your pop socks when trying on skirts and dresses. They look awful!

Don't wear too many clothes when you go out shopping. You'll get hot and bothered in overheated shops and you will have too much to take off each time you try something on.

Try things on – don't guess!

Troubleshooting

Beating the Festive Freeze
George Wingfield; Andy Greenfield; Simon Mitchell; The Institute of Plumbing; The National Association of Plumbing; Peter Baker

Plumbing problems

If you are away during the Christmas period, make sure your home doesn't suffer from a sudden freeze.

Insulate the attic, put an insulated jacket around the cylinder and lag the pipes.

Some small heaters operate safely in a roof space to prevent pipes from freezing, but check with your electrical supplier or electrician.

Protect outside taps and pipes by covering them in straw.

Keep heating on low while you are away. Heating bills will cost less than an emergency call-out.

Make sure your boiler has been recently serviced. Boilers are under greater pressure during this time, when a house is occupied more and the weather is cold.

Keep your gutters clear of leaves and debris, and check the roof flashing.

Keep a stock of salt or grit for paths, especially at the top of a slope, so that you can spread it out as you descend.

Thaw pipes as quickly as possible after you discover they are frozen.

Leave the main water supply valve open. Incoming water pressure will help remove loosened ice.

Start at the tap when thawing and work towards the source.

Use one of these methods to safely thaw a pipe:
- *Place hot-water bottles* over the pipes.
- *Use an electric hairdryer* to blow warm air directly on the suspected frozen area.
- *Use an infra-red heat lamp* directly on the suspected frozen area. For added efficiency, place a piece of sheet metal or aluminium foil behind the pipe while heating.
- *Pour boiling water* on the pipe after wrapping rags around the suspected frozen area. However, this method is slow and messy and may take many gallons of water. *CAUTION: Boiling water can cause serious scalds. Be extremely careful when transporting and pouring boiling water.*

Never use a blowtorch to thaw frozen pipes. This is the cause of most of the home fires that are started when trying to accomplish this task.

Always know where the main stopcock is. If you have an emergency, like a burst pipe, you will need to get to the stopcock quickly. If you don't know where it is, put this book down and go and find your stopcock – *now*. Try looking under the kitchen sink.

Make sure your stopcock is in good working order. When you have found it, make sure you can turn it on and off. To turn it off, go clockwise; you will have done it properly if no water comes out of the kitchen tap when it's turned on. If you can get water from the tap, the washer probably needs replacing.

Ensure that your stopcock doesn't jam. Open and close it several times a year. When you have opened it, give it a quarter-turn clockwise. This should stop it jamming without interrupting the flow of water.

To clean out a blocked loo pan, use an old string mop. A couple of plunges should do the trick.

To stop an overflow from your cistern, place a wooden spoon across the cistern and tie the lever arm, attached to the ball float, to the spoon. If you need to flush the loo, you will have to release the arm to fill the cistern. Tie it up again when you have finished.

To clear blockages in sinks or basins, cover overflow holes with a damp cloth to build up pressure while you use a plunger.

If a pipe has split, wrap torn strips of fabric tightly around the leak, put a bucket underneath to catch any drips and call a qualified plumber.

Use a spanner that's the right size rather an adjustable wrench to avoid damaging the taps.

If a spanner is too big, you can introduce a shim to make it the right size – use a feeler gauge from a car, or a 5p piece.

Put a cloth over a valve that you're bleeding to prevent mucky water staining the walls, the radiator or you.

Out and about

To avoid falls in cold and icy weather, wear thinner-soled shoes if you have poor circulation or loss of feeling in your legs and feet. These will help with better traction and better sensitivity to the surface you're walking on.

If arthritis and sore joints are a problem, use thicker-soled shoes to cushion the impact of walking and give you greater support.

Wear sturdy, low-heeled shoes.

Be especially careful on stairs. Always use handrails.

Don't walk in a hurry. Falls most often occur when you're walking faster than usual.

Plant care

Spring- and summer-flowering house plants are dormant during the winter, but you can keep them and flowering ones alive while you are away. A week or so before your trip, put them in a room with indirect light and turn off the heating in the room.

Cover the floor of the room with newspapers and plastic and place all your plants on it together in a group.

Open curtains or blinds to allow optimum light to enter the room. Make sure that your plants aren't in draughts.

Check the room's temperature before you leave so that there is no sudden drop when you are away. The ideal temperature is in the low to mid-50s during the day, falling to the upper 40s at night. In this range, your plants will survive without extra care for a few weeks.

Water all plants the day before you leave, whether they need it or not. Let pots drain fully.

If you don't have a room that you can set aside for the plants, try leaving them in the bathtub. After soaking them well, cover them with a light sheet of clear plastic and they'll survive for 2 weeks or longer.

If you are leaving them in the bathroom, turn off any heating so that the room will remain cool and the plants won't dry out.

You can also use self-watering wicks, which are available in most garden centres.

In the garden, don't worry about a light, freshly fallen snow. It's an excellent insulator if frigid weather follows.

Smaller, younger plants have a harder time surviving the cold than larger plants. Be sure to protect these during icy weather.

If you have plants that have been attacked by insects or diseases, pay special attention to them during the winter.

De-icing salts can be toxic to many flowers, trees, shrubs and grasses. When de-icing pathways and driveways, be careful not to get the substance too near plants or grasses.

Healthy Christmas
Dr Guy Richards; Dr Kate Crocker

Breath smell of garlic or onion? Chew parsley, and floss your teeth.

Bad breath can be the result of poor elimination of waste from your body – so for a couple of days eat a diet high in fibre, fresh fruit and vegetables.

Digestive problems

Unfamiliar and rich food can cause stomach upsets in young children. Cut back on sweets, creamy and fried foods and see if it helps.

If you tend to get bloated when you have overeaten, avoid wearing 'control' underwear (favourites during the party season) as they put pressure on your abdomen. Try massaging your stomach in a clockwise direction with a few drops of ginger essential oil mixed with a carrier oil.

Peppermint tea will also help to relieve trapped wind.

For hiccups, try a teaspoon of vinegar.

Upset stomach? Drink plenty of water to avoid dehydration (a solution of 1.5g of salt with a teaspoon of sugar stirred into a glass of water works well).

For nausea and vomiting, sip diluted, unsweetened lemon juice.

Hangovers: prevention and cures

To avoid feeling drunk, eat as you drink – especially fatty foods and carbohydrates – and follow every alcoholic drink with a glass of water.

Before drinking take a couple of capsules of cynara (artichoke extract) with an apple to stimulate liver function. Available from chemists.

Or drink a pint of milk and eat some bread before you start drinking.

Prevent hangovers by eating a spoonful of coleslaw before bed. (Honest!)

Drink 2 pints of water before going to bed to avoid a hangover (which is chiefly caused by dehydration) in the morning.

Help a hangover with a couple of spoon-fuls of honey which will raise your blood sugar level; then take a couple of high-dose vitamin B and C tablets (alcohol destroys these vitamins in your body).

If you have over-indulged, take milk thistle tablets to help your liver to process toxins.

Disaster prevention

Clear half-empty glasses away to make sure young children can't get their hands on alcohol.

Nuts can cause choking in young children, and even allergies, so don't leave trays of nuts where they can reach them.

Make sure small parts of new toys aren't easy for young children to eat or stick up their noses or in their ears.

Emergencies

Christmas lights cause 1,000 accidents a year. If someone receives a shock, break the current – switch it off at the mains – and push the person clear of the current with a stick or broom handle (not anything metal). Dial 999.

If you burn yourself, run the affected part under cold water for 10 minutes.

After a bad burn, take 1g of vitamin C every hour for 2–3 hours. Vitamin E cream or aloe vera gel will also help to relieve burns.

For your medicine cupboard

Paracetamol
Soluble aspirin (but not for children under 12)
Ibuprofen/paracetamol syrup
Antiseptic solution/cream
Indigestion remedies
Rehydrating salts
Thermometer
Mild laxative
Plasters
Dressings
Triangular bandage
Disposable gloves
Cotton wool
Safety pins
Tweezers
Eyewash
Bandages
Eyepads
Eyedrops
Scissors
Condoms

Dental Emergencies
Claire Baines; British Dental Association

If a first tooth is knocked out, leave it. It would soon have come out on its own anyway.

If a second tooth is knocked out whole, try to reimplant it immediately, making sure you get it the right way round!

If you can't reimplant it, store it in some milk and see a dentist immediately.

If no milk is available, tuck it inside your cheek, up next to the gum, and get to a dentist straight away.

To reduce discomfort from sensitive teeth, try applying some desensitising toothpaste around the base of the tooth and to the gum after brushing, and leave it there.

If you have a broken tooth and can't see a dentist over Christmas, you can minimise scratching to the tongue and the inside of the mouth by taking a little piece of wax from an Edam (or similar) cheese, rolling it up and placing it on the jagged tooth.

You can temporarily fix a broken-off crown back in place using sugar-free gum or denture fixative.

If you have toothache, an anti-inflammatory painkiller, such as ibuprofen, will give greater pain relief than paracetamol.

Don't put crushed aspirin around a sore tooth – it can lead to an 'aspirin burn' inside the mouth.

For abscesses, don't place a hot-water bottle against your face, as it's likely to lead to a build-up of more pus.

If you have an abscess and your face is swollen, hold hot, salty water inside your mouth to encourage the abscess to drain into the mouth. Spit, rinse and repeat.

Remember to organise repeat prescriptions well in advance of the Christmas holidays.

Catastrophe Christmas

www.howtocleananything.com; Kerry Pencaster; Maggie Baker

Run out of margarine and eggs to make a cake? Use mayonnaise. It works just as well, and makes a very moist cake.

If the heating packs up, most people find heavy clothes uncomfortable indoors. Thermal underwear is ideal for keeping you warm and comfy.

Persuade everyone to dress in loads of layers. Try to make it a game to persuade children to join in.

Knitted silk underwear is very warm and light and can be found in ski shops.

A fleece jacket is warm without being heavy and doesn't look daft worn indoors. Better-quality ones will keep you warmer. Get one that unzips all the way, rather than one you pull over your head.

Keep the extremities warm, because the circulation is that much slower. Two pairs of socks are a minimum requirement.

Cook the turkey on the barbecue if all your power fails. Put it in on its baking tray, well wrapped in foil, and put the lid on the barbecue.

Before Christmas, make sure you have plenty of ice (even get a large bag from the fish counter at the supermarket where it is free) and have it on standby in the freezer in case the power goes and you need to keep food cool.

Power cut? Try to open the fridge and freezer as little as possible. Food will stay cold and/or frozen for a surprisingly long time.

Stains, marks and spills

When someone has spilt water on your furniture: get rid of white residual marks by making a paste of baking soda and water and rubbing it on the marks. They will disappear. Use wax polishing and scratch remover to restore the sheen.

For burn marks on furniture: depending on how deep the scorch marks are, you may very well be able to sand off the damage and refinish the table. Make sure that it is a solid wood table and not particle board covered with veneer.

Try these techniques:
- **Start by sanding the surface** of the table in the area of the damage. In theory, you should go over the entire surface equally, but as long as you remove the finish from the entire surface, even if slightly more material is removed where the burn marks are, no one is likely to notice the imperfection.

- **Once the blemish is removed**, move to a finer sandpaper, and sand the entire surface. If you are uncertain of matching the existing finish (colour and gloss), you should sand the rest of the piece as well (legs, sides, etc.) and refinish the entire table. Before finishing, and usually between finish coats, sand with a 220 grade sandpaper. This should leave a perfectly smooth finish.

• **Wipe the table with a rag** to remove all of the dust, and refinish in a well-ventilated and dust-free environment. Use lots of thin coats of finish, not one thick one.

Spills on upholstery: a quick cleaning tip is to fill your sink with water and washing-up liquid, and allow the soap to really bubble. Wipe the upholstery, using only the bubbles, with a clean white towel. This will remove surface dirt, but it is not an effective deep-cleaning method.

Remove the stain as soon as it is noticed. Use a clean white, absorbent terry towel to blot the stained area, cleaning the stain from the edge to the centre.

If you are using a commercial product, apply cleaner to the towel or cloth first and test an inconspicuous area of carpet. Use modest amounts of cleaning solution.

Remove the dirty excess before cleaning and use cleaning compounds at lukewarm temperature.

Don't use a dirty or coloured rag, and don't rub, brush or scrape the spot using force.

When someone spills red wine on clothing or tablecloths, simply pour enough good white wine over the stain, let it soak in and rinse out with warm water.

To remove wine stains from a carpet: a quick tip is to pour salt over the spill and allow the wine to soak into the salt. Then vacuum up the salt. Try using white wine on red wine, as in the technique above, but most effective is to blot up as much of the wine as possible, then treat as you would a coffee spill.

Rub a potato on to a stain. The enzymes in potatoes will help remove it.

A French treatment for a red-wine stain is to pour mineral water over it, but do it quickly. Tap water too can sometimes do the trick.

When all else fails, the French remove difficult stains by rubbing with a damp block of soap and then laying the item in the sunlight. It may take a day or so to work (and there may not be much sunshine at Christmas). You can also try stretching the stained area of fabric over a bowl and pouring boiling water through the stain. Don't use this method on delicate fabrics.

To remove candle wax from a carpet: chip off as much as possible first. Lay a terry towel on the wax, then take an iron (on medium heat) and place it on the towel. This will enable the wax to wick up into the towel. Be sure to keep inspecting the towel as you work, and continue moving to a fresh or

clean area of the towel until the wax is gone.
Dyes in candles can cause permanent stains.
If a stain remains once the wax is removed,
treat it as a dye stain.

To remove coffee stains from a carpet:
try to get to the stain as quickly as possible.
The longer the stain is left on the carpet, the
greater the chances are of it setting. Remove
all excess liquid by blotting with a terry towel
or kitchen paper. Mix half a teaspoon of mild
hand-wash detergent into 8fl oz warm water.
Apply a small amount, blot and repeat until
the stain is removed. Be patient. Complete
removal may require repeating the same step
several times. When blotting, press down on
the carpet, but do not scrub, as this may
distort the texture of the pile. Cover the stain
with the towel and press down repeatedly to
absorb the stain material and detergent.

Once the stain is completely removed,
rinse the area with cold water; blot with a dry
white terry towel until all moisture is
removed. Repeat this process several times to
remove cleaning solution residue. (Residue
can attract dirt.)

Never use laundry detergent or automatic
dishwashing detergents on a stain because
they may destroy or dye some fibres.

**If the spot or stain turns brownish when
it has dried**, mix 1 part white vinegar and 2
parts water. Apply a small amount and blot.
Repeat only once.

If the dog pees on the carpet in all the

excitement, cover the wet area with soda water, then absorb the moisture with clean towels.

Cigarette smells: smoke, of any sort, permeates into the pores of all surfaces and leaves a residue that will cause the odour to linger. Try to air out the room often and for extended periods of time. It is amazing how much this can reduce the smell. Light a candle (especially a scented one) to help disperse the odour. If it lingers, you will need to wash all the upholstery.

Remove the smell of smoke from clothes by hanging them in the bathroom when you have a shower. It will help steam out creases too.

Remove burn marks from a wool carpet when grandpa falls asleep with a cigar in his hand, by rubbing the burn immediately with a slice of potato, which will take the singe out of the surface. The brown tips can usually be washed out or discreetly trimmed with nail scissors.

An old wives' remedy for cleaning embroidery: sponge on a mixture of 225g (8oz) soft soap, 225g (8oz) honey, and 20fl oz (1 pint) English gin. Rinse off well. (Vary the amounts, depending on the quantity that needs cleaning!)

Discover a stain at the last minute on the tablecloth? Cover it with rose petals, and sprinkle more around the table to make a feature!

For grease stains on clothes or uphol-stery, sprinkle on plenty of talc and leave for a good 10 minutes. Brush off lightly and the grease should come away with the talc.

Essentials for Christmas

Trawl the local paper and make a list of plumbers, electricians and doctors' surgeries that are open during the Christmas period. Emergency call-outs for plumbers and electricians can be enormously expensive. Be warned but don't be conned.

Don't forget list:
Foil – extra-wide for the turkey
Extra-large roasting tin for the turkey
Enough plates and glasses for guests
Dishwasher tablets
Paper napkins
Kitchen paper
Clingfilm
Greaseproof paper
Baking parchment
Bin liners
Freezer bags
Frozen basics (milk, butter, bacon, fresh pasta, bread)
Coffee and tea
Ice
Light bulbs
Matches for lighting the fire and igniting the brandy on the Christmas pud
Candles (for effect, not just for power cuts!)
Coal or logs for open fires
Loo paper
Sticky tape
Extra wrapping paper and gift cards
Camera
And film
Batteries for toys
Extra presents for unexpected guests

Getting Over It

Post-Festive Recovery

Lynne Robinson, www.bodycontrol.co.uk; Harriet Morgan; Caroline Armstrong and Dave Scott, Nike

Shake off over-indulgence and winter blues by making sure you have enough zinc and vitamin C in your diet. Both will help boost your resistance to bugs and flu, which can hit you after the Christmas holidays.

Don't try to lose the pounds you've put on over Christmas by missing meals. Your body will slow down, trying to save your calories for a famine.

A little chocolate is a comfort that can lift your mood. Also try bananas, which are calming. Avocados, chillies and pasta can make you feel more upbeat.

Walk each day in natural bright daylight to relieve winter blues. Lack of sunlight can affect your mood.

Don't be fooled by low-sugar foods. A gram of fat contains 9 calories, which is twice as much as other foods.

Try to cut out alcohol for January. Drink sparkling water, real fruit juice or herbal teas.

Running

Buy decent shoes: go to a specialist running shop and have your feet properly measured.

Don't skimp on the price either. You'll never regret it.

Avoid running in cotton T-shirts, which get wet, cold and heavy. Get yourself into moisture-wicking fabrics (such as hi-tech sports fabrics designed to keep you cool) and you will be a whole lot more comfortable.

If you have bigger legs, wear cycling shorts or running tights to stop your legs chafing together as you run.

Warm up before you set out running. Not only will it stretch your muscles, but it means that you won't have to wear a sweatshirt or other top. (You won't want to have to carry extra gear with you, once you have been running for a few minutes.)

Run with a Walkman or Discman. It has been scientifically proven that music can affect sporting performance. Listen to music you like while you are running and you will not only feel better, but you will achieve more and exert less energy. The reverse applies with music you don't like.

But remember that running in headphones will mean you won't be able to hear traffic or someone coming up behind you.

If you're prone to getting a stitch, avoiding eating or drinking for up to 1 hour before you run.

Run with a partner, especially if you are female and especially in the winter when it gets dark earlier.

Start slowly. Walk briskly for a couple of minutes, then jog for a couple, then go back to walking again. Go on like this, gradually increasing the jogging and reducing the walking, until you can run for 20 minutes without getting too puffed to talk.

Just starting running? Don't try to be too ambitious. Try to run several laps that pass your original starting point. That way, you won't have such a distance to go back if you become tired.

Stop running if you injure yourself, become dizzy or get very tired …

However, don't stop if you are only a bit tired. You need to push yourself to improve. Just stop and walk for a bit until you get your breath back.

You need to run for 15 or 20 minutes before you even begin to burn off calories!

If you do get an injury, have it treated by a professional. It won't get better if you just ignore it – it will get worse.

Post-Christmas health drive? Wear thin layers that you can shed and tie around your waist. Be careful of ice and run only when the light is best.

Take plenty of fluids on board – even if you don't think you need them. By the time you think you do, it will be too late. You will already have started to dehydrate.

Try to train for a big run with a group. It will keep you motivated, even when you're not in the mood, and you'll find you don't even notice the difference.

Workouts and aerobics

Start each workout with a few minutes' relaxation.

Clear a space before you start – you don't want to have to keep stopping to move furniture.

The best time to exercise is in the late afternoon or evening when muscles are already warmed up. If you exercise in the morning, you'll have to spend longer warming up.

Clear your mind and focus on your body as you exercise. Concentrate on each movement and on relaxing the parts of your body that aren't involved.

Having strong pelvic floor muscles is *so* important. Some people have trouble isolating them but if you suck your thumb as you squeeze, and concentrate at the same time on drawing up the muscles inside, you should have no problem!

Cross-patterns in exercise are good for your brain as well as your body. Any kind of movement where the left arm is moved at the same time as the right leg, and vice versa, will do.

Exercise instructions can be complicated. Try taping yourself reading them out and work along with the tape. Be careful not to read too fast!

When using arm weights, start with half-kilo weights and work up gradually to 2 kilos. You can improvise weights with a bag of rice or dried beans.

Small cans are fine for starting resistance work, but don't use big ones in an effort to increase the weight. If they're too big, your hands will strain to keep hold of them.

Add sneaky exercises to your daily routine – do pliés while you make the packed lunches, leg raises while cleaning your teeth, clench and release your buttocks while on the phone and squeeze your pelvic floor at traffic lights.

Climb stairs two at a time for a great bum toner.

You can do standing push-ups against a door frame. Stand in the doorway, then take a step back. Place your hands against the door frame at shoulder height, then bend your elbows and smoothly straighten them again. Start with 5 repetitions (or reps) and work up from there.

Step-ups on the stairs are not quite as effective as a step class, because you can't vary the direction of stepping, but they can help to raise your heart rate. Be careful you don't wear a hole in the carpet.

Index